IS IT COZ I'M BLACK?

IS IT COZ I'M BLACK?
NDUMISO NGCOBO

Published by Two Dogs
an imprint of SchreiberFord Publications

•

SchreiberFord Publications
PO Box 50664, The Waterfront, Cape Town, 8001

info@twodogs.co.za
www.twodogs.co.za

•

First published 2009
Reprinted 2009

3 5 7 9 8 6 4 2

•

Publication © 2009 Two Dogs
Text © 2009 Ndumiso Ngcobo

•

All rights reserved. No part of this publication may be reproduced, stored
in a retrieval system or transmitted, in any form or by any means, electronic,
mechanical, photocopying, recording or otherwise, without the prior
written permission of the copyright owners.

•

Publishing director: Daniel Ford
Managing director: Grant Schreiber
Publishing manager: Tim Richman
Art director: Francois Pretorius
Illustrations: Dominique Beukes
Proof reader: Ania Rokita

•

Distributed by Quartet Sales & Marketing

Printed and bound by Tandym Print, Park Road, Western Province Park, Epping, South Africa

•

ISBN 9781920137250

More Dobermanns

About the author

Ndumiso Ngcobo was born in Mpumalanga Township, Hammarsdale, west of Durban. He has worked as a mathematics and science high-school teacher, held a variety of positions in the food-manufacturing corporate world and worked as a technical consultant.

Nowadays, he spends his days writing books, articles, columns and television scripts. He is the author of the acclaimed *Some Of My Best Friends Are White*.

He lives in the Ekurhuleni Metropole of Gauteng with his wife and three children.

Contents

- Introduction · 9
- The Amish Of The Joburg 'Burbs · 13
- The Xenos Are Coming! · 25
- Jou Ma Se Passion Gap · 35
- Come Off It! You Would Kill For Julius Malema… · 45
- With This Gall Bladder, I Thee Wed · 55
- The Afrikaner-Americans Of The East Rand · 67
- Honk If You Feel Your Taxes Aren't Working For You · 79
- Music: The True Opium Of The Masses · 95
- No Sex, Please! We're Calvinists · 107
- Of Phallic Traditional Weapons And Estelle Getty · 119
- The Hunchback Of Howard College · 131
- The Church Of Thirst And The Beard · 143

Is It Coz I'm Black?

Introduction

Dear Reader

In 2007 I wrote a book entitled *Some Of My Best Friends Are White*. The official description from the creative types at my publishers' marketing department described it as "a collection of satirical essays" about the "idiosyncrasies" of our nation from a "successful corporate professional" and whatnot. Up until that point I had not even been aware of the existence of the word "idiosyncrasy". I also hadn't realised that I had been successful as a professional in the corporate world. Be that as it may, from my point of view, I still insist that it was just a collection of random hallucinatory thoughts.

The reason I mention *Some Of My Best Friends Are White* at this point (other than the transparent plug) is that this book would not exist without the relative commercial success of that one. At one point it didn't look as if it would sell more than 23 copies a month, but slowly it got going and next thing my publisher was telling me I was a "minor celebrity".

The question I have been subsequently asked more than any other during newspaper, magazine, radio and television interviews has been this: "Did the success of your book surprise you?" Depending on my levels of truthfulness on the day in question, I have given varying answers that can be summed up as, "Well, yes and no". But the no-bullshit truth is that I didn't expect it to appeal to as many people as it did. I underestimated South Africans' collective readiness to laugh at themselves when mocked and ridiculed.

And so *Is It Coz I'm Black?* is an unabashed continuation on the same theme. It is another collection of random thoughts about people and situations specific to South Africa that I find fascinating, paradoxical or downright absurd.

Compiling this collection was far more challenging than writing the first one. My first challenge was an uncertainty about whether or not to go the same route as before. Smarter, more experienced individuals cautioned me against the danger of painting myself into the "satirist" corner. This was another unexpected revelation about my writing that I wasn't quite prepared for: the "satire" tag. I just might be the world's first recorded case of an accidental satirist. It seems that even when I try hard to write with a straight face, someone is always bound to giggle and act all childish about it.

In any case, at some point during my "meditation", I seriously considered following up with a collection of fictional short stories that I have been writing in my spare time. But through a complex process involving deep introspection, ignoring the advice of others and imbibing copious amounts of quasi-expensive hard liquor, I came to the conclusion that following up and "completing" some of the thoughts and themes that emerged in the first book was a good idea. Plus, I figured that a collection of fictional stories from me at this stage would be a bit like Mandoza following up *Nkalakatha* with a gospel album. And that would be rather confusing and undesirable.

My second challenge came with the realisation that when I was writing the first collection of essays I had not really been aware that the thoughts I was putting down would eventually end up in a book. You can appreciate the disparity in self-awareness between that book and this one. Back then I was just a bored corporate slug whose only qualification to write was the fact that I could work a keyboard on account of my opposable thumbs. While I was writing this one I was constantly self-conscious about the words I was putting down. Am I repeating myself? Am I exaggerating this section for shock value? Is this bit withstanding the truth test? Does anybody care?

Then there was writer's block. Writer's block, my third challenge, is perhaps the most painful calamity to befall anyone who fancies him or herself as some kind of writer. I had a brief taste of the dreaded blockage in the midst of writing this very masterpiece. It is a feeling not too dissimilar to constipation. Fortunately for me, it lasted not much longer than about three days. I was sitting there staring at the blank screen when I had an epiphany. My revelation occurred to me in the form of a midget mosquito that whispered in my ear, "Oke, who do you think you're kidding? You'll never experience the sensation of an original thought passing through your brain." Once my mind was cleared of the foolishness of chasing the original-thought fantasy, the words came at the pace of Noah's floods. Do not underestimate just how ill-advised the desire to be intelligent, lucid or relevant can be. It is a no-win situation for most of us whose names are not Stephen Hawkins.

This does not mean that I have given up on the Holy Grail that is original thought. As a matter of fact, I often wake up in the middle of the night, switch my PC on and type deep incisive thoughts on a blank document. Suffice it to say, come morning when I re-read the "gems" I came up with at 3.37am, they are a bit… well, the opposite of whatever original is. I think that the most original idea I have had in the wee hours is something along the lines of, "There is strong evidence that the Pope might be Catholic." I actually wrote these words in the belief that I was breaking some new ground not too long ago. But because I'm a member of pound-for-pound the most superior species in the universe, I will soldier on in pursuit of the Grail.

Enjoy the original thoughts…

NN
March 2009

Is It Coz I'm Black?

The Amish Of The Joburg 'Burbs

When a friend of mine purchased his first home about five years ago, he promptly handed over a set of house keys to me for safekeeping. This way, he reasoned, if he should inadvertently part ways with his own set, it wouldn't be necessary for him to have to engage in transactional sex on Oxford Road just to have a roof over his head for the night. Great thinking on his part since he's a notorious drunk – as are most of my friends.

Recently, this particular friend put his house on the market. Yes, yes – he's quite aware of the global economic meltdown and this being a buyer's market and whatnot. He's selling because he's moving to a different province altogether and doesn't need the hassle of maintaining a stand-alone house from 250 kilometres away. So he calls me the other day and asks me to go to his house to get some documents for him or wash his socks or something – I can't really remember. Anyway, I drive there, open the gate, park the car and walk into his house. And all hell breaks loose as the alarm siren goes crazy. Most South African prisoners – otherwise known as homeowners – know this audio cue. It is one of the most terrifying sounds you could ever hear. A house alarm circumvents the eardrums and auditory nerves and goes straight to your belly. It strikes the fear of God into any ordinary person. The problem being, from what I've heard on the urban-legend circuit, that burglars are never much bothered by house alarms. Apparently some have been known to prioritise stealing your iPod first so they can casually walk around your house looting at will with Mandoza blaring in their ears to drown out the noise. But I'm no burglar, despite having given some serious thought to cleaning out my perpetually inebriated friend during these trying economic times. Now back to the story.

So I put down my beer and mumble to myself like John the Baptist in the wilderness: "Calm down. You saved the alarm code somewhere on your phone." And sure enough, there it is. I casually stroll over to the alarm control station – read: I bolt towards it like a yellow-bellied zebra with a pride of rabies-infected lions in hot pursuit – and type in the five-digit number. Nothing. I type it in again. The siren winds up to a more feverish pitch. Panic sets in. I can picture those simple security bastards in SWAT uniforms who live for blowing things away shining red laser beams on my melon already. The size of my head pretty much makes it a no-miss target for these highly trained snipers with post-1994 rage burning inside them. Bullets of sweat are pouring down my face. Type-type-type-type-type. Nada. Finally I call the sonofabitch owner.

"Oh," he says, "I meant to tell you but the control keypad isn't working."

My relaxed response: "But what do you mean it's not working? How do you switch it off? And more importantly *FERCHRISSAKES CALL THE ARMED RESPONSE GUYS AND TELL THEM TO STAND DOWN!*"

After what seems like an eternity while I'm executing intricate NASA-esque electronics stunts, the sirens die down. I feel sick to the pit of my gut. My bladder has shrunk to the size of a fruit fly's and I feel a desire to relieve myself. Expeditiously. But I'm not hanging around the house of siren hell, so I step outside, close the door firmly behind me and do my business right there on my alcoholic friend's immaculate lawn. My contribution to the nitrogen cycle…

I guess I could go on regaling you with the rest of the story and how, just as I was leaving, his bitch escaped into the street and how I had to chase her around for 25 minutes but I think you'd reach your boredom tipping point pretty soon. And no, silly, I mean his Ridgeback.

The point of this long and rambling anecdote is to hone in on our national obsession with crime and security. You will notice that I didn't include "safety" in that last sentence. That's because I have always had a bone to pick with the naming of that cabinet portfolio, the Ministry of Safety and Security. I've always (mis)understood the meaning of the word "safety" to be confined to protection against accidents and unintentional events – generally unfortunate things that we bring upon ourselves. And I've always just assumed that the true value of the fat guys in tight-fitting blue polyester uniforms is to provide "security" for the public; that is, protecting us against the evil intentions of the bad guys out there. I think putting in that "safety" aspect of things in the name was a sneaky way of

The Amish Of The Joburg 'Burbs

weaselling out of their true duty. Instead of protecting us from criminals, the police seem content merely to protect us from ourselves. You can see it in their priorities. Just walk around the streets with a quart of beer in your hand and marvel at the efficiency of the Safety gurus as they descend upon you like fireflies on a fluorescent condom in the dark. Of course, the world is not a better place because an idiot who may or may not have perished in a hit-and-run "accident" is safely behind bars. In fact, it can be argued that the gene pool has been weakened by allowing him to live. Meanwhile, the guys who make their living by acquiring your car off you at the intersection down the street are left to go about their business.

And so you have a bunch of guys heavily steeped in enforcing laws that are designed to protect the individual from accidental harm such as crashing their cars, suffering acute alcoholic poisoning, overdosing on crack cocaine and suffering heart attacks in shady brothels. That's why there are so many police officers who look like they couldn't run from here to the gate without collapsing from hypertension and heat exhaustion. The last time I was inside a police charge office I was getting an affidavit after someone relieved me of the burden of carrying my wallet around (what with all those bank cards, driver's licence, cash and so on). A thought occurred to me while I was there: not one of the members of the Big Five behind the counter could catch me over any distance of more than ten metres. And I'm a porky out-of-shape guy myself. Perhaps it is out of the desperate realisation that the police force is made up of overweight fatties who couldn't catch a granny with a walker that Gauteng MEC for Safety and Security, Susan Shabangu, called on them to "shoot to kill". Too many bad guys getting away. I see the Johannesburg Metro Police Department has tried to circumvent the slow-metabolism problem by purchasing dozens of bicycles. Just the other day, I witnessed a bevy of female JMPD coppers taking their bikes out for a cruise on the M2, thunderous thighs and bottoms spilling out on either side of their straining bike frames. Had my left hand not been otherwise occupied with a cold beverage, I might have snapped a picture with my phone. Alas.

Faced with this skewed focus on drunks, hookers and other exotic forms of vagrants that seems to occupy every waking minute of the fatties in blue, worrying about security has fallen into the laps of the ordinary citizen in South Africa. And some sections of the population have taken on this mantle with the obsessive feverish eagerness of Deborah Patta sniffing a whiff of government corruption. I have argued before that the levels of crime in this country are completely out of hand. Indeed, they are surpassed only by our over-the-top obsession with crime. Let me say it out loud: we have become downright paranoid and hysterical about crime.

A few months ago I was in a car with two gentlemen: a visiting Dutch national and a South African fellow who was behind the wheel. I was struggling to understand my countryman's choice of the longest possible route from Boksburg to Krugersdorp until he mentioned to the Dutch fellow that the quickest route was via the N1 but then that would have caused us to drive past Soweto. The lateral neurological pathways in my brain are legendary for their ability to connect the disconnected yet I was failing to comprehend what the problem was.

"Have you had a bad experience in Soweto?" I enquired in confusion.

"Are you crazy?" he responded. "I have never been inside Soweto!"

Inside Soweto. Not *to* Soweto but *inside* Soweto. I was reminded of the insightful someone who pointed out to me that you always drive *into* Soweto, *into* Alexandra and *into* the Joburg CBD. It's quite normal to hear someone say, "I sometimes drive into Khayelitsha." Never *to* Khayelitsha. But you don't drive into Wynberg or Sandton. You drive *to* Wynberg and *to* Sandton.

It hit me that, in this man's mind, Soweto is not all too dissimilar to a dark abyss – a kind of black hole. You just have to drive *past* Soweto and the crime will quite possibly suck you right in. The poor man's eyes almost popped out of his skull when our Dutch companion pointed out to him that I would be taking him to a few Soweto shebeens the following day. Admittedly, I had embellished the shebeen part of the tour to the Dutchman. We ended up on Vilakazi Street and hit a popular Rockville *shisanyama* just outside The Rock pub/club afterwards. But it was worth it just to see the reaction from my Boksburg-to-Krugersdorp-via-Pretoria friend, who had clearly demonstrated the type of thinking that is, I believe, at the very core of why our national obsession with security is ineffectual and, quite frankly, retarded.

Our security measures do not satisfy the basic tenets of logic. The first line of defence against car theft is the standard alarm system and immobiliser that our insurance companies insist we all have installed in our cars. So the bad guys decide, "To hell with it, we'll just take your keys from you." Enter a variety of intricate, state-of-the-art electronic anti-hijack devices. So the bad guys decide, "Well, we'll take your car and yourself so that you can disconnect it for us." So the security companies get even more technological and give us those "smart" tracking devices that can tell the control rooms when something is amiss with a person's normal behavioural patterns. Of course, for abnormal people such as myself with no discernible pattern to speak of, this is a useless technological breakthrough.

All of this is a classic case of treating the symptoms and ignoring the root causes. As a result, none of these incredible inventions are making the slightest dent on the rate of crime. You might think that I am immune to this madness, the way I'm carrying on. Oh no, I am a poster boy for this very idiocy. I, too, have every security gadget imaginable, including the run-of-the-mill house alarm complete with armed response.

Just the other day, my wife, kids and I went out to my four-year-old's favourite fast-food outlet to complete his birthday celebrations. Before you could say Mc-take-a-bite, the phone rings. The alarm in the house has just been triggered. Ten minutes later we're weaving through suburban streets averaging 150km/h, putting toddlers on tricycles in danger in our haste to arrive home… to do what exactly? This is the thought that races through my mind as I screech to a halt outside my house. No sign of the bulky guys in SWAT uniforms. So, do I go inside and get bludgeoned to death with the corner of my own laptop by a guy with a Mandoza iPod? Or do I wait outside twiddling my thumbs? I feel ridiculous standing outside my own house, scared to go inside, waiting for someone to say everything is okay.

In the end, nothing was amiss; no-one had broken in. Perhaps one of our "pets", the vermin that skulks around your typical suburb, tripped the alarm. Blame it on the family of woodpeckers that lives somewhere inside our roof. Or maybe it was the armed-response guys just having some fun. Who knows? And it's a story that's probably happened to everyone out there who's ever had a house alarm.

Meanwhile, we continue unrestrained on our path of security obsession. And you have to wonder about some of the measures we take to feel secure. I have a bunch of friends who are doctors at one of our health facilities. Each time I go in I have to sign my name and inscribe other personal details, including my ID number, mobile number, car registration and penile length. I don't know why, considering the security guards never ask me to give them a missed call to ascertain the veracity of my number. Nobody asks me for my ID book, either, to verify my ID number. Nobody ever follows me to the urinal to see… I suppose it's for them to be able to say, "The guy who raided our blood bank was a short, stubby guy who answers to the name Kofi Annan and he can be reached on 082873442975558 – hey, check it out, he's got a 15-digit number! That's cool!" Of course, by that time I'll be long gone with my loot of intravenous drips and hypodermic syringes, yelling "Yee-haa!" into the sunset. I guess it's one of life's childish pleasures signing any old crap on those tattered forms. When it suits me, I'm Mvuyelwa Mbeki, and when I'm having a cranky whine-about-the-ANC day, I'm Mpilo Tutu. Hell, I've even got away with being Hashim Amla, despite my lack of fuzzy beard.

And don't you just love the serious look the security guards give you right before they ask you to open the boot – you know, just in case you're transporting Jimmy Hoffa's corpse in there? Never mind the fact that this high-level protector of this high-calibre institution is armed only with a torch, handcuffs and a Bic finepoint pen in his shirt pocket. I guess the modus operandi is to blind would-be criminals with the torch and write "Bad, bad man" on their foreheads so they can be identified when the police fatties come around later to handcuff them to those big dog houses

The Amish Of The Joburg 'Burbs

where they sit all night drinking tea. It's the same nonsense I'm always subjected to when I check in at the airport.

"Sir, are you carrying any sharp objects in your bag?"

"No, ma'am. To hijack the aeroplane, I think I'll use the stainless-steel knife you'll hand over to me as soon as I sit down. If that fails I'll break the wine bottle and threaten the pilot with that."

"Carry on."

And of course the madness doesn't stop there. There is that whole industry of people who make their money by transporting other people's money. I always look at these vehicles with "Cash in transit" signs boldly emblazoned on the side panels and wonder. I mean, is it possible to attract more attention than this? Isn't this a lot like walking in the street with a T-shirt that reads ABOUT R3,500 CASH RIGHT HERE! with a nice big arrow pointing to your shirt pocket? Everybody can tell which vehicles are carrying insane amounts of cash so why advertise it?

And then you're minding your business in a mall when suddenly these crazy people are all around you with their bulletproof vests and more guns than Arnold Schwarzenegger in *Terminator III*. When I see these guys standing outside a bank I'm going to, I always turn around and head for the nearest pub to wait it out. Hell no! I listen to the radio every day and I'm not going down like that! Never mind that these nervous, twitchy bastards are as highly strung as that yellow-bellied zebra we met earlier. I don't want to walk past them, inadvertently trip on my laces and die a gory death in a hail of bullets.

If we're lucky and we survive the attempts on our lives by the carjackers, burglars and the cash-in-transit guards, we might earn enough money to afford to live in security complexes, estates or gated communities. People who argue that the human race is not evolving any more have clearly not been to one of Joburg's gated suburbs. There's a sorry bunch of people right there. To begin with, they always claim something along the lines of, "Since we've fenced the area in, crime has decreased exponentially." Every time I hear this statement I catch the unmistakable whiff of cow dung. It just doesn't smell right. I don't see how hijacking syndicates are deterred by torch-and-Bic bearers at the entrance of these tragic army barracks. I think the real reason they fence in their suburbs is because hordes of dark people milling about make some people nervous. Hey, I understand. Five brothers walking towards me in a deserted street always makes *me* nervous. Just call a spade a shovel.

But more than that, I think living inside an enclosure is a pathetic way to live. This is why I have personally resisted the urge to move to Pennsylvania and join an Amish colony, despite the awesome life that the Amish lead. There is just a certain discomfort I feel whenever I visit one of these places. I always wonder how long it will be before all males in the compound are required, by community ordinance, to start wearing a black-and-white uniform and keeping a long, moustache-less beard to easily identify residents from intruders. People in these communities are obsessed with who is a resident and who is not. Not so long ago, I was visiting a friend in one of these "villages" and I decided to take a walk. A lady who looked like she was in her eighties accosted me with righteous indignation. She had one of those crazy eyes with a disconcerting oscillation. She peered at me and hissed, "Are you a resident here?" with the authority of a town manager or at least a council member of the *Ordnung*. I was going to respond in my usual flippant manner – "No, I'm just scoping out a house I'm going to burgle later" – but something about her told me to hold back. I got the feeling she hadn't been to the "outside world" in years and might not get my humour. So I mumbled something about being late for my gardening job and hurried along.

But mark my words, it's only a matter of time before members of these communities are debating issues such as how many suspenders the men should display, whether unmarried women should wear bonnets or not and whether nailing half-sisters during the *Rumspringa* – that is, the period of adolescent debauchery among the Amish, so you know – is acceptable.

If it sounds like I'm making light of the crime situation in the country, it's probably because I am. The situation is dire enough on its own. There is no need for all of us to suffer unnecessary anxiety attacks and die from

The Amish Of The Joburg 'Burbs 21

strokes. There certainly is no need to cower behind fences, living an endogamic existence and risking the Ellis van Creveld syndrome in one's offspring. I think the solutions to our crime-ridden nation need more creativity than an expandible security gate with deadlock mechanisms.

In the meantime, I have made a personal decision not to be petrified by crime. If I'm going to live in this sunbathed semi-arid wilderness I call home, then goddamnit I'm going to enjoy the sun. As a result I take all the necessary security precautions I can, such as rolling up my windows and locking my doors when I go out. (Apparently hijackers are petrified of rolled-up windows.) But I go out as much as I please. And I go everywhere. I'm one of those guys you find in *shisanyamas* on Sunday afternoons listening to Afro-jazz blaring from car boots. But if you decide to skulk around in your back garden for the rest of eternity like the Amish, that's cool too. You know where to find me if you decide to come out.

The Amish Of The Joburg 'Burbs

Is It Coz I'm Black?

The Xenos Are Coming!

Like most self-respecting black men – which is to say, not Dali Tambo or the Honourable Reverend Meshoe – my hairstyle of choice is the cheesekop: a good old clean-shaven skull. For me, this decision means that I never have to disgrace my proud manly forefathers and visit a girly hair salon. I have my melon shaved either at a taxi rank or a hostel, killing two birds with one stone in the process. Firstly, I delude myself into believing that I'm maintaining my street cred and, secondly, I get to soak up some kassie culture – all for about a tenth of the price of an emasculating designer cut in Sandton. And please note that I'm bringing up my coconut kids the same way, twang and all.

When I was a little boy, my father introduced me to the township barbershop. He used to take my brothers and me to a man called Bab' uMbona, possibly the most unkempt individual I have ever laid eyes on. I have seen Rastas and Shembes with neater beards, which is quite an indictment considering I used to hang out in Hillbrow every day at one point in my life. Bab' uMbona had a typical township barbershop, although the word "shop" is a bit of an imaginative stretch. His shop, for want of a better word, was situated under a peach tree in his yard. It consisted of two unsteady wooden benches, a car battery for power supply, two hair clippers, a shoe brush and a couple of filthy stinky rags that I suspect had previously been Mrs Mbona's pinafore in her vetkoek business.

You'd typically arrive and sit in the sun waiting for Bab' uMbona to finish cutting someone else's hair – and then wait a few more minutes while he decided whether you were worthy of his attention. If his favourite team, AmaZulu, had lost (again) that weekend he'd be in a mean mood and your ass would be toast. He'd grab your head roughly, inspect it with the disdain of a vet inspecting a stray mutt, and bark, *"Yini sengathi unezintwala wena mfana?"* [Boy, do you have lice?] And then the scalping would begin. I have seen gentler haircuts in an Australian sheep-shearing contest. Any successful endeavour requires a specific target. Bab' uMbona's target was to see how many nicks and cuts he could impart on your head by the time he was done. If you were lucky you would escape with about 20 per cent of your scalp's surface area still intact. And then, with more gashes on your head than a guy wearing a VIVA MANDELA T-shirt at an IFP rally, Bab' uMbona would douse your head with methylated spirits, presumably to kill off any lice still keen on making it their place of residence. I personally think he flooded my head in methylated spirits because he was a closet Nazi sadist who got off on nine-year-old boys' girly screams. This "service" would cost the grand total of R1.50 – a rather steep fee in 1981 – whereafter Bab' uMbona would let me escape his catch-and-release "shop", to stagger outside, half-blind from the methylated spirits and smelling of Mrs Mbona's fish-and-vetkoek combo.

The whole barbershop industry was turned on its head round about the time of the return of the exiles. The first time I entered a barbershop owned by a Congolese national in downtown Joburg, I thought I'd inadvertently stumbled into a plush brothel. For starters, his shop was inside a tent – so no methylated spirits running into your eyes due to an unforeseen cloud burst. And the floor was carpeted. There was an actual bench with a wide mirror for me to marvel at my physical magnificence. The barber was well-dressed and smelt like he'd taken a Turkish bath. His hands were manicured and he was clean-shaven. There was something suspiciously… human about him. He was courteous, asked me to tell him if his clippers pinched and made chitchat in broken English. Okay, so the pompous turd boasted about Congo's win over Bafana Bafana the whole time, but still, I was impressed.

When he finished, he rinsed my head in lukewarm water and applied some scalp cream and talcum powder. I was so overwhelmed I almost asked if he offered "happy endings". And he charged me what all the other Bab' uMbonas on the same street charged – about R5 at the time. I think it's fair to say that if the real Bab' uMbona had witnessed this scene, he would have discharged his lunch on the spot. I had discovered heaven.

For the next few months, I regularly returned to Marko's tent for more pampering – until the bubble burst when some Bab' uMbona types attacked him, beat him within an inch of his life and he fled Joburg. The year was 1994. The next time I saw Marko was in 2005 at Durban

International Airport. He didn't remember me, naturally. But in the brief two-minute conversation we had, he told me he was running four hair salons in and around Durban. I wanted to ululate.

In the aftermath of the first wave of 2008 attacks on "foreign" African immigrants, I drove to the Dunswart taxi rank in downtown Boksburg for a haircut. (Yes, Boksburg is a big enough city to have a downtown.) These days the shaving of my skull is shared between Bab' Nzama from Watville hostel in Benoni, Jeremiah from Daveyton taxi rank and, as on that Tuesday afternoon, the Mlungu brothers at the Dunswart taxi rank. Lucas and Phillip Mlungu are Tsonga-speaking siblings who hail from the south of Mozambique but have been living in South Africa since the late '80s. They tend to be quite vague about the exact town/village they come from. To this day, they are still rather suspicious of people who ask too many questions about their origins – it's a Renamo/Frelimo thing, I think. Either way, I have been having my head shaved in their makeshift tent for the last seven years now, and on this particularly day, after the bloodiest weekend of the "Kill amakwerekwere" orgy of stupidity, I rocked up at their barbershop.

Lucas was there but Phillip wasn't. I tensed up. Careful not to betray my anxiety, I casually inquired as to Phillip's whereabouts. He was okay, came the reply. He was just moving some of the brothers' things to a safer location to pre-empt any attacks on the settlement they were staying in. It was a strained conversation, very different from our usual free-flowing talk about how the mighty Kaizer Chiefs had won yet another trophy while the Pirates drought was now in its sixth season. On this day, our chat was intermittently interrupted by a variety of Zulu-speaking taxi drivers:

"*We-Sbali, bafuna ukuniqeda abantu. Yekani ukukhulisa imithondo bese nidla abafazi babantu kodwa nani.*"
[These people want to kill you. Maybe you should stop growing your dicks so long and fucking their women.]

"Hawu Sbali, ngiyathokoza mawusaphila. Ngibone isithombe somuntu onombombo ocijile ephepheni ngathi 'Yeka ngoSbali bakithi'. Phela umuntu mayesha akabonakali kahle."
[I'm so glad you're still alive. I saw a picture of a burning man in the paper and, to my dismay, his brow looked suspiciously like yours. It's difficult to tell when a man's on fire.]

"Umfazi wami kunini engitshela ukuthi angisebenzise i-Ambi. Njengoba nginsundu nginje, sengiphilela ovalweni manje ngoba angazi noma bazothi ngiyiShangane yini manje nami."
[My wife has been telling me for years to use skin-lighteners. Look now, I'm perpetually stressed that people will think I'm a Shangaan.]

And so on it went, amidst guffaws of laughter. To a complete stranger to the taxi-rank world, these utterances may have sounded callous and disgusting, considering the shameful events of the previous week. But to those of us who hang out there regularly, it wasn't anything out of the ordinary. It is not uncommon to someone at the south end of the rank to shout at someone on the north side, "You smell of unwashed shebeen whores!" Or, "There's a woman peddling dick-growing concoctions over here. Come quick!" Or, "Your nose looks like the stitch on a scrotum." (Until that point, I hadn't even realised it was stitched but when I checked I was amazed. I believe my exact words were, "I'll be damned!")

This is all my way of illustrating that the taxi rank is a vicious brutal place without space for sensitivity. So the inappropriate "jokes" about this human tragedy did not sound out of place. I expected nothing less. If anything, the crude and insensitive banter was actually a way for people to awkwardly communicate the fact that they were distancing themselves from the madness. Humour is the vehicle they employ to relay uncomfortable messages.

What sheer madness this whole thing is. My use of the present tense is a way of pointing out that the attacks on immigrants of African descent were not the one-off "event" or "episode" that most people seem to think.

The Xenos Are Coming!

We have been down this path of retardation many times since the very first trickle of immigrants from neighbouring African countries.

You will notice that I have not used the "x" word that is in vogue when this subject comes up. I violently disagree that the orgy of stupidity we witnessed in Alexandra, Thokoza and other places was a manifestation of xenophobia. Let me put it this way: if people in this country were xenophobes, Kaizer Chiefs' Turkish-German coach, Muhsin Ertugral, would be considered a kwerekwere just like his former Orlando Pirates counterpart, the DRC's Bibey Mutombo. Each time Pirates lost under Mutombo, I would hear the words, "This kwerekwere is messing up the team," or something to that effect – even though the record will show that Pirates' results improved when Mutombo took over.

So if it's not xenophobia, what is it then? Well, the answer is a simple one: it's racism. Ninety-nine per cent of the victims of the inappropriately named "xenophobic attacks" are Mozambican, Zimbabwean, Somalian, Congolese or West African. People from the rest of the world – from the UK, Western Europe, Eastern Europe, the Middle East, the Far East and pretty much everywhere else – were not harmed during the creation of this madness. No-one could care less that David Bullard was born in England. He's no kwerekwere.

One thing I've been arguing for a while now is that everybody's racist. The whiteys can't stand anyone who's not white. The Asians hate everybody. The French would nuke England if they could get away with it. The English think the Irish are savages. The Russians wish the Ukrainians would just die off already… The world is just one huge big orgy of hatred. But of all groups in the world, I think black people are worse off than everyone else. And yes, I know that black people are not one homogenous group. Try to work with me here. The reason I think black people have got it worst is simply this: black people hate other black people too. Sure, the Afrikaners might hate the souties, but they won't *really* hate their own.

If you're black, tell me that this hasn't happened to you. You're nonchalantly minding your own business in the supermarket, looking for some lime cordial or something. The next thing you know there's a hissing sound emanating from the lips of a cleaning lady standing next to those CAUTION: WET FLOOR signboards, *"Wemntanami, wahamba langisula khona kodwa!"* [My child, why are you walking where I'm working?] Dead stop. You look around perplexed at all the whiteys and Asians stomping all over her wet floor at that very moment. A United Nations of stomping. Yet the only person she has a problem walking on her shiny wet floor is you.

Or, as my wife likes to point out, the car guards. She loved telling me, during her last maternity leave, how she'd emerge from the mall pushing a trolley laden with nappies and other infant-related goods. The car guards would just look at her demurely while she struggled with her trolley, unpacked the groceries into her boot and walked the trolley back to the trolley bay. Yet when a white tannie came along, 12 car guards would re-enact the Matebeleland massacre, fighting for the right to push her trolley and unpack her goods. Initially she thought it had to do with the fact that perhaps black people are lousy tippers. But then, over the weeks, she kept on parking at the same spot each time she went to the mall and she began to realise that even if she gave the same car guard R10 each time around, he'd still prefer a R5 coin from a whitey. I see it in the way my car-guarding brethren will call me, a black man, *mlungu wami* or *ngamla* [both colloquialisms for "whitey"] as a sign of great "respect". It's the type of thing that makes me want to go all Jet Li on people and roundhouse kick them in their Adam's apples.

The most popular excuse I heard during the attacks on nationals from neighbouring countries was that it was "a symptom of poorly educated people getting frustrated with the government's poor service delivery". My response to that was "bull bollocks". I've worked in a multinational corporation. I've watched foreign nationals from the UK, the Netherlands and Germany trickle into the company to take up senior positions without a hitch. All good. And I've watched the reaction of my professional colleagues with degrees when a foreign national from Ghana or Cameroon walked through the door: resistance from day one. It slowly dawned on me that this whole thing was really symptomatic of a deep self-hatred for

The Xenos Are Coming!   31

people of the same appearance. If it was really about xenophobia, there would have been a stampede at the airports as the British nationals fled the marauding mobs.

A while ago, I wrote a blog on the *Mail & Guardian*-hosted Thought Leader website. To quote myself:

"Now here comes the obligatory preachy bit. It may seem that I am treating this serious matter in the same fast-food, flippant manner with which I treat everything else. And perhaps I am guilty as charged. But I just cannot help myself. All I ever see is the absurdity that is inherent in any situation. I'm just another human idiot and I'm just tweaked that way.

"I think that history will judge our root-cause-analysis skills very harshly here. We're busy fiddling while Alexandra burns – literally. But for as long as immigration is seen as a 'problem' that the government must tackle only where immigration pertains to people of Zimbabwean, Mozambican, Nigerian and Congolese extraction, to name a few, we're just a bunch of irrational idiotic racists. The whole lot of us.

"Most of us who are here were immigrants at some point. What is the cut-off date for being a legitimate South African? Let's not hide behind technicalities about who is here legally and who is not. Quite frankly, that's a sideshow. Deep down in places that people don't talk about in polite company, people just hate that people cross these presumably very legitimate borders and try to make a life for themselves. Even if not a single crime in South Africa were attributable to a Zimbabwean, people would find other excuses. But we never deal with these issues honestly, do we?

"I wish people would just say what's on their minds; that they wish that the Nigerians, Zimbabweans, Somalis would just go home – ignoring the fact that people tend not to find any reason why the Eastern European, Indian, Chinese, British or any other kind of immigrants should leave. Then some of us would start wondering if this was pure xenophobia or xenophobic racism or racist xenophobia. From people of all colours. And then we would have a jolly good time engaging in South Africa's favourite pastime: bickering about it. I cannot even begin to imagine how fascinating the exercise of figuring out who came from where and when would be."

Sure, I was sounding all serious, but I fully stand by those words.

Is It Coz I'm Black?

Jou Ma Se Passion Gap

I am a mixed coloured.

I know. I also used to delude myself into believing that I was a short porky black African man who hails from the Kingdom of the Zulu. But self-delusion is my thing. Before I got married I also had delusions of grandeur about my sexual prowess. Only stifled giggles from my wife put me straight.

In any case, a couple of years back I was attending a relative's funeral in the small town of Verulam, north of Durban. At some point my younger brother and I are standing in line to honour that famous African tradition of dunking one's hands in cow dung after the burial when we are accosted by a posse of middle-aged coloured females. One of them is a distant aunt of ours I had met at previous family gatherings. After the customary greetings, she turns around to introduce us to her companions: "These are Cousin Rosemary's sons, Auntie Margaret's daughter. You remember her, mos? From the mixed-coloured side of the family?"

My brother's jaw hit the floor with an almost audible thump. Had my hands not been preoccupied with gathering up my own mandibles from the dust, I might have gone to his assistance. "Mixed coloured." I had never heard that expression before. Neither have you, I'd venture. Like most people, I have always been under the ostensibly ignorant assumption that coloured people were mixed enough as it is. Even more fascinating was to follow: as the unmixed-coloured auntie of mine threw in the "mixed coloured" bit into her introduction, she gave us that proud, conspiratorial look that said, "I've got your back. If you just go along with it, nobody here will know you're black. Not on my watch." It wasn't as much a derogatory statement as it was a little nudge up the rungs of the social ladder. A little complimentary upgrade from Auntie Purity from the untainted-coloured side of the family. Wink wink, nudge nudge.

The more cynical reader will see right through this seemingly innocuous little "mixed-coloured" anecdote. One of the major challenges that satirists and other humorist types face is how to ridicule people without offending them. I have found that the most effective trick is to brainwash the target of your mockery into believing that "You and I are the same. So when

I mock you, I mock myself too. I'm not laughing at you. I'm laughing with you." So, for instance, if you're going to ridicule Orlando Pirates fans it would probably be a cool gimmick to wear a ridiculous hard hat with a skull-and-bones crest, stand alone in a half-empty stadium and bawl your eyes out. Pirates fans like doing that sort of thing and calling it passion. And I think that my mixed-coloured story adequately serves that purpose. It entitles me to talk as much shit about coloured people as I want to. After all, some of *this* mixed coloured's family are actually "pure" coloureds. And if my cow-dung-queue tale weren't true, I most certainly would have made one up. We call that literary licence in the business. I plan to use my family privilege wisely.

The only reason I'm even writing about coloured people is because of the unbearable pressure I have had to endure from legions of coloured folk. Since my first collection of hallucinatory ramblings was published, I've had coloured people from all walks of life confront me about their exclusion from that book. "Why must everything be about blacks and whites? Shit, you even had the charas in your book! Are we boeshies so insignificant in this new South Africa that you can't even poke fun at us?" And I'd look around nervously. Coloured folk using the word "poke" always makes me shift uneasily. Blame it on the year I spent at the Natal University Alan Taylor Residence in the Durban South coloured township of Wentworth almost 20 years ago.

The residence primarily housed medical students, some of whom ran a free clinic for the community. I remember sitting in the clinic waiting room one Sunday morning. Long story involving an itchy groin after a liaison with a female of questionable moral convictions. Don't judge me. Scrawny 17-year-old first years with only R4.75 in their bank accounts have been known to scrape the bottom of the barrel to curb the evils of sperm-retention syndrome.

But I digress. Back to those poking coloureds. So I'm minding my business at the clinic when two breathless coloured youths burst into the waiting room. Both of them are covered in blood from a gaping wound on the upper arm of one of the young men. Judging from the potent fumes

Jou Ma Se Passion Gap   37

emanating from their pores, I'd estimate that they'd probably consumed about 13 bottles of rather cheap brandy between the two of them. The bleeding young man seemed extraordinarily preoccupied with the time it would take to have his arm stitched up by the student doctor.

"Don't worry about it. I'll have you stitched up in no more than ten minutes," came the response from Mac, who was on duty that morning.

"Please doctor, man. Make that two minutes. I want go back quick-quick and poke the fucking dog that poked me," came the legendary response.

I am not shy to share the fact that I suffer from many personality disorders. One of these is my strange aversion to research. Or any other endeavour designed to cure me of my notorious ignorance. But what I think sets me apart from your run-of-the-mill ignoramus is that I have never been known to allow my boundless ignorance to stand in the way of sharing my ignorant opinions with others.

So when my coloured friends pleaded with me to poke (figuratively) fun at them, I threw myself at the task with the fervour of a Pentecostal preacher on the pulpit on a month-end Sunday. When I started, all I had were a few anecdotes, not unlike the ones I have already shared. Since this was a special project that needed extra effort, I signed up as a user on a website called Bruin-ou.com which describes itself as "the only portal about South Africa's mixed-race people". Most of you would call that internet surfing. I call it extensive research.

The very first article I encountered upon entering the website was titled "Wentworth becomes a war zone again". And the very first sentence read as follows: "The shots rang out soon after 1pm on Saturday last week, and many of us ran out of the barracks – blocks of flats next to the Engen refinery – to find yet another teenage corpse…" My first observation is that the barracks that the author is referring to used to be the Alan Taylor Residence where the famous poking teenager got stitched up. My second observation is that the story had familiar themes. Gangsterism. Violence. Drug abuse. Nightclubs. Alcohol. Council flats. And, of course, apartheid-era town planning.

The themes were familiar to me because I had sent out a "questionnaire" to a few friends asking them to give me stereotypical words and phrases they associate with coloured people. The same themes as above emerged. The rest of the words included the terms "Ma se poes", "naai", "Ricardo", "passion gaps", "tik", "cabbage bredie" and so on. This reminded me of something that one of the uncouth uncultured scum I call my friends told me a couple of years back. He comes from Mitchell's Plain in the Cape Flats. Let's call him Stevland – mostly because that is his real name.

Stevland says that one of the most fascinating sights one is likely to experience in the Cape Flats is a gun battle between rival gangs. In any other place the street would clear at the speed of light at the sound of the first shot. Not in Mitchell's Plain, he says. Apparently you're quite likely to see a middle-aged woman in hair rollers and a nightie, despite it being three in the afternoon. She will probably be standing inside her gate with a baby in one arm, barking instructions to her son who is taking part in the shooting battle.

"Daar gaan hy! Skiet hom dood, Denzil! Skiet hom!" [There he goes! Shoot him dead, Denzil! Shoot him!]

I'm not making this up. Stevland is.

I must say that reading through the articles, blogs and exchanges in the chatroom on Bruin-ou was a bit of an eye-opener. Most coloured people I know on a personal level have a strong disdain for stereotypes about coloured people. A lot of them do not even identify themselves as "coloured". Rather, they prefer to be called "African" or simply "black". There are also those at the opposite end of the spectrum who like to call themselves "bruin Afrikaners". I've also heard that phrase "so-called coloured" – with the obligatory index finger raised in the air – bandied about a lot. I've often found myself chuckling privately, imagining someone calling himself a "so-called German" or a "so-called person". This is the paradox of living in South Africa.

Then there are all the arguments to the effect that the coloured race is a nonexistent, made-up bullshit concept and "everywhere else Barack Obama is not coloured but simply black". But these are arguments from

Jou Ma Se Passion Gap **39**

intellectual types who have read too many books. I prefer to call them snobs. I don't like these types of coloureds. I dislike them as much as I dislike black dashiki-wearing pan-Africanists. You probably know the types I'm talking about. They're the ones who will spot me planning my escape from a BEE do, seal off the room, trap me in a corner and proceed to lecture me about the dangers of stereotyping African people. For eight hours. The torture normally doesn't end until I have been regaled with the history of Mapungubwe and had various books by Chinua Achebe shoved in my face. Indeed, I find these guys as irritating as the snobbish "intellectual" coloureds. These are the types of people who mess with my quest to mock and ridicule everybody.

I'll tell you which coloureds I like, though. I wonder how many black people have had this happen to them. I often approach the deli section at my local Pick n Pay and find it manned by a coloured auntie. However, it's not always possible to tell who is coloured and who is black. After all, I might be more light-skinned than Benni McCarthy. In these cases, I will get to the front of the queue and order my pepper-steak pie in isiZulu or broken SeSotho. When auntie inevitably responds indignantly in the thickest most-Cape-Flats accent she can muster just to set me straight about her identity, I always thank the Almighty for the free entertainment. With the price of movie tickets these days, entertainment is an expensive hard-to-come-by thing. I call such moments the good times.

Sometimes when I'm in Cape Town I'll go to the deli section even when I don't really feel like a pie or chicken wings just to mess around with the darkest-skinned auntie I can locate. The darker ones are usually the most righteously indignant ones; the most likely to call you "jou naai" when you get there and start ratting off in isiXhosa. The expression on their faces is often priceless. It's an expression I like to describe as such: "My name is Dolores February. How dare you confuse me with a Xhosa woman? Can't you see that I have straight hair that generations of Februarys used to befuddle the apartheid regime by passing the pencil test?" And then I giggle myself silly in the private knowledge that I have saved myself R50 on a movie ticket. This is the coloured I like; not Ursula

Stapelfeldt, with all her pseudo-sophisticated *Top Billing* airs. Ursula would not call me "jou ma se poes" if I addressed her in isiXhosa. She looks like the kind who has taught herself some pidgin Xhosa of sorts. She would probably smile and respond good-naturedly before sheepishly apologising that this is the only Xhosa she knows. This is not the coloured person I appreciate.

But there is a snobbish coloured I do like: the educated but non-intellectual coloured. Some years back when I was still a single man on the prowl, I went to a nightclub in Rosebank with a few buddies. We were all in the type of predatory mode that can only be brought about by consuming copious amounts of whisky. Pretty soon I had pinned down a female I believed was mostly likely to go back to my pad for purposes of swapping bodily fluids. My biggest hurdle was her brother-in-law who kept growling at me menacingly. I could see that he was struggling to contain his desire to open a pressurised can of whupass on my black ass for wanting to defile the gene pool with my inferior Zulu DNA. After all, it takes generations of careful matchmaking before a proud coloured mom can boast to her friends, "My Jerome is so faaair and his hair so straaaight!"

But because I had turned the charm dial all the way to maximum I soon found myself on the dance floor with Jerome's sister-in-law, performing the usual retarded courtship ritual. So far so good. But after an hour of gyrating our hips against each other, I was getting a little impatient. I needed to work quickly because it was already 2am and I could see that my buddies had had fruitful hunting and would be leaving soon. My own negotiations were not going so well. My "date" was a tad too concerned with the fact that I didn't seem appreciative enough of the awesome deal I was getting with her.

She kept on repeating her academic qualifications to me. Okay, so she's a dentist. Cool. I didn't mind the repetition – I was, after all, plying her with a steady supply of Spiced Gold doubles. What finally drove me over the edge was that she kept on rubbing her bosom against me and sensuously whispering, "So, have you ever had a woman of mixed genealogy before?" This happened, oh, about 300 times a minute. Mixed genealogy. Big words inside a nightclub at 3am. Needless to say, when I got home, I only had my pillow to hug. But the mixed-genealogy gem had been worth me heading home alone and having to resort to the one-armed struggle against sperm-retention syndrome.

Another coloured I like is the middle-aged coloured dude who is the life of every work party. You know the guy I'm talking about, right? He's always the one who volunteers to go first at the Christmas karaoke party. And there are no prizes for guessing what he'll sing. Correctomundo! Nat King Cole to break you into the free old-school concert you will enjoy for the next five hours. By the time he's done you will have heard Marvin Gaye, The Temptations, The Manhattans and every soul group you've ever come across. Some of the team members are a little shy to go up on stage? Fear not, Gareth is here to save the day!

You know why I like this type of coloured dude? Because Gareth does not fear the perpetually happy celebratory-coloured stereotype. You've probably heard the old joke from apartheid days. The one about the very clear division of labour during the struggle, where the whiteys would do all the thinking and strategising, the Indians would organise all the finances, the darkies would do all the toyi-toying and die in numbers – and the coloureds would organise the booze for the celebration afterwards.

I do not know whether stereotypes about coloured people are deserved or not. I do not know whether stereotypes about the new inductees into the coloured family, the Chinese, are deserved either. Hell, I do not know if *anybody* deserves stereotypes about themselves. There aren't enough years in one lifetime to fulfil one's ambition to drink as much beer as possible *and* waste time researching these things. Perhaps those who believe that the very existence of a coloured identity is ludicrous are correct. Maybe they are right when they assert that people who hold on to a coloured identity are embracing an outdated, artificial, divisive and irrelevant apartheid-era stratification.

I tend to hold a different view. I believe that the right of an individual to assume whatever identity he is comfortable with supersedes any other rights. I do not quite understand why people expend so much energy castigating others for embracing identities that suit them. Coloureds, so-called coloureds, Africans, bruin Afrikaners, boeshies – who cares? I certainly don't.

If anything, I like the fact that a people who were lumped into one category hold such diverse identities about themselves. That appeals to me. I think there's a lesson in there the rest of us can follow. Our job is to watch and learn something. And mock and ridicule, of course. After all, some members of this diverse church have been known to knock out their front teeth using a baksteen.

Is It Coz I'm Black?

Come Off It! You'd Kill For Julius Malema...

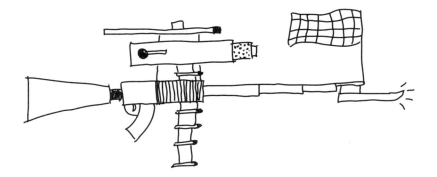

I have a tendency to worry about things I shouldn't really worry about. A resident of the Sterkfontein Mental Health Facility recently assured me that the only reason there hasn't been a cut in the global gravitational supply is because while we sleep he keeps it in check. That and the fact that Eskom doesn't supply us with our gravitational needs, presumably. Such assurances worry me more than they should comfort me. You have no idea how often I have nightmares about all currently earth-bound things floating off into space yonder. Imagine being kept as a sex slave in a Martian harem. As we all know, Martians are a sexually depraved bunch, what with their propensity to stick probes up Alaskans' poop holes. Well, all Alaskans except Sarah Palin, of course…

You'll probably agree that this opening paragraph is a good example of "far out" thinking. You may even call it crazy if you want. But do you know what worries me even more? It is the fact that my levels of irrational worry are still below the national average. I swear South Africans have the most highly developed "worry for absolutely no reason" propensity in the world. Take our whole obsession with Julius Malema, for instance. In the unlikely event that you're not South African (read: totally irrelevant in the greater scheme of things), allow me to put you in the picture. Julius Malema is the ANC Youth League (ANCYL) president whose greatest claim to fame is that he once took one drag too many from the bong before a political rally and ended up saying that he was prepared to take lives on behalf of ANC president, Jacob Zuma. Unnecessary statement, I know. Especially considering that Zuma probably has an impressive stash of machine guns by now (assuming that his followers have occasionally heeded his melodic pleas to be supplied with automatic weapons).

Malema took over the ANCYL presidency from the marginally less controversial Fikile Mbalula whose own claim to fame is being the most prominent *mkhwetha*, or Xhosa initiate, in history. Both of these characters follow in the footsteps of a long and auspicious line of fiery ultra-militant ANCYL presidents, including one Nelson Rolihlahla Mandela. History seems to have glossed over Mandela's own spurious bungee jumps into the depths of militant rhetoric and hotheadedness. That's right, Nelson Mandela had an insatiable penchant for blowing shit up when he was the ANCYL president. And this is by his own admission in his biography. That is just the traditional role that the leader of the ANCYL is supposed to play: figure out what the official party line is and exaggerate it. Good cop, bad cop, anyone? I really feel silly pointing this out, but it seems to be something that really needs to be specifically stated.

Remember Peter Mokaba and his "Kill the boer, kill the farmer" chant? Does anybody *really* believe that Peter Mokaba fancied crawling over sheep droppings in one of his famous Dior shirts to kill Jannie van Tonder on the outskirts of Phalaborwa? If you believe this, may I suggest that you too have, of late, been taking hits from the bong? And may I also suggest that if you're a Wynberg housewife and you think Julius Malema's over-the-top agitating-for-votes statement was "deplorable" and worthy of the attention of the HRC's Jody Kollapen, you also need to lay off the weed? No? Okay, let's perform a little experiment.

You know that panic button you keep on the inside of you brassiere as you go around the house supervising Mavis's chores? Press it right at this moment. Now, how many seconds do you think it will be before those willing-to-kill-for-Mrs-Wynberg ADT guys arrive with the stealth of Dan Brown's Hassassin and splatter any would-be-burglar's brains all over your gardenias? When you say, "But that's different", all I'm hearing is, "Well, he started it." Real mature. So, let's talk about who started the orgy of violence that is a part of our everyday lives, shall we?

According to the Genesis of the Judeo-Christian-Islamic religions, Adam's son Cain started it all when he got pissed off that his dad liked his younger brother Abel's arse-licking more than he liked his. Since then, subsequent human beings have followed suit. Your neighbour has great fire-starting rocks? Kill him and get those rocks. The neighbouring clan has better grazing pastures? Kill them and drive the survivors off the land. Africa has gold, diamonds, titanium and stuff? Invade the continent and kill and colonise the locals. And, as a human race, we celebrate those at the forefront of such behaviour and bestow upon them great accolades.

We've even been known to name countries, capital cities, streets, months of the year and dilapidated football stadiums after them. From Pharaoh Ramses II to Achilles to Julius Caesar to Shaka kaSenzangakhona to Rocky Malebane-Metsing, that subjugator of Lesotho, we celebrate our great conquerors. Yet when an aspiring conqueror – Julius Malema – emerges and makes it known that he is planning a bloody putsch, we call Jody Kollapen. To quote Eric Qualen from that enduring movie *Cliffhanger*: "Kill a few people, they call you a murderer. Kill a million and you're a conqueror."

Most people I know would not agree with the statement "I would pay trigger-happy people on steroids to kill other people on my behalf." That doesn't surprise me. But Mrs Wynberg thinks that the R499.95 (including VAT) that ADT takes from her account every month pays only for the snazzy uniforms, worryingly shiny boots and those intimidating Ford Bantams. Apparently the 9mm Parabellums with laser-beam sights are in the Incidentals part of the budget. Fair enough. But you can't fault her logic because you also call yourself a pacifist who is right royally appalled by Julius Malema – and yet… Well, let's see what you did.

"You" took about R30-billion, give or take a couple of Rooivalks, from the 2008/2009 fiscus and deposited it into the Ministry of Defence's coffers. This to fund an army that has not been in any actual war since Jan Smuts's brown-nosing exercises during World War II. (Well, that's if you ignore the Magnus Malan-inspired suicide missions in places like Cuito Cuanavale that were, let's be honest, entirely unnecessary.) Yet you put on your Sunday best, nodded eagerly at Trevor's every word during his budget speech and concurred with his decisions, using important-sounding phrases like "balanced budget". Thirty billion rand. That's roughly the original value of the arms deal that Patricia de Lille has been screeching about for what seems like several centuries. In just one financial year. Put another way, R30-billion is roughly ten times as much as Ethiopia spends on defence in a year. And the Ethiopians have an excuse. They are involved in a prolonged low-intensity war with their neighbour, Eritrea, over borders and whatnot. (For a visual, just imagine a tense dispute over virgins between Mswati III and Goodwill Zwelithini on the Ngwavuma side of the border between Swaziland and South Africa.)

If you're an active citizen it might interest you to know where all of that R30-billion for Defence is going. Of course, if you're an enterprising individual in the mould of Patrice Motsepe you're probably seeing an opportunity and thinking to yourself, "There must be a government tender in there somewhere."

In any case, the rationale for this spending was provided by then Minister of Defence the Honourable MGP Lekota, before he became a turncoat in the national democratic revolution. In his address during the Defence 2008/2009 Budget Vote he started out by harking back to 1994, explaining how the apartheid-era army (as run by the previously mentioned chrome-dome Magnus Malan) had been in an "offensive defence posture" leading up to 27 April 1994. Translated into English, this intricate technical Defence Force language means "killing people just for the heck of it". He then went on to explain that since the whole democratisation process, we had adopted a far more palatable form of killing folk: the "defensive defence posture" – essentially shooting people through the oesophagus only if they started it. This is sometimes known as "peacekeeping".

To quote the erstwhile Honourable Minister: "A big part of the budget goes to peacekeeping and peace enforcement." Peace enforcement. I like hearing shit like that. The idea of enforcing peace gives me hope for the future of the human race. It harks back to my favourite utterance by a South African revolutionary, Harry Gwala. During a particularly heated speech at the Natal University Students' Union Building, circa 1990, he let rip with this gem: "People who do not want peace will have peace imposed upon them through the barrel of a gun." Man, did that mess with my head! I kept conjuring up images of disarmed guys in fatigues hanging their heads in shame, all peaceful and contrite for daring to stand up to the Lion of Pietermaritzburg.

If you really want to understand what keeping defence forces is all about, you have to give this message a bit of thought. It's about killing

Come Off It! You'd Kill For Julius Malema... **49**

enough of the bad guys to dissuade the rest from even thinking about it. "Peace enforcement" effectively boils down to killing people because they started it. Because they deserve it – like Mrs Wynberg's burglar who perishes in a hail of bullets on her freshly laid bed of gardenias.

One of the greatest cinematic examinations of the complications of violence comes from the pen of one David Webb Peoples, the man who wrote the script for *Unforgiven*, which was directed by and starred a certain Clint Eastwood. After the Eastwood character, William Munny, guides a young man called the Schofield Kid through his first killing, the following exchange takes place:

> *The Schofield Kid:* It don't seem real how he ain't gonna never breathe again, ever. How he's dead. And the other one, too. All on account of pulling a trigger.
> *William Munny:* It's a hell of a thing, killing a man. Take away all he's got, all he's ever gonna have.
> *The Schofield Kid:* Yeah, well, I guess they had it coming.
> *William Munny:* We all got it coming, kid.

I like that. I like hearing that I'm not the only one who deserves to have someone place a Kalashnikov against my temple and squeeze the trigger for about 20 uninterrupted seconds. I've often felt that I deserved it when I've rolled down the window at an intersection to allow my R200-a-gram-sirloin-generated flatulence to escape – next to a taxi with 16 people getting by on R50 a day. By any rational natural law, anyone who spends R600 on one meal while children die scavenging through rubble for a 50-cent slice of bread deserves to die a cruel and excruciatingly painful death – for the good of mankind. Nothing about that behaviour says "survival of the species". Especially when that person has the audacity to blame the government for the plight of that child after listening to a news bulletin on a Bose system in his R450,000 vehicle. That's the epitome of an individual who deserves to get shot because "they had it coming", I reckon.

South Africa, like most other nations, was built on a solid foundation of killing people en masse, piling up their corpses on a spit and dancing around their charred remains like wild banshees. It is just our way. Only people who've been sipping on some pretty concentrated Obama juice have problems with this fact of life. You don't think there are 11 million Zulus in this country because Shaka went around chanting "Yes we can!", do you? Sorry to disappoint but, to paraphrase Harry Gwala: "People who do not want to make peace with iLembe [Shaka] will have peace imposed upon them through the metal part of *iklwa* [spear]." And this is how it came to pass that my people, the AmaQadi, became Zulus, circa 1820.

In the event that you are hallucinating and believing me to be glorifying the use of violence, let me assure you that I am not. I'm just pointing out that since the beginning of time we humans have been killing each other to bend the wills of others to our way of thinking. You think I'm typing this in English because Lord Shepstone made a rousing "Yes we can!" speech on the summit of Isandlwana to convince King Cetshwayo's Unokhenke regiment to put down their amabheshu and wear pants instead? I'm just pointing out what is – not what should be.

Speaking of Isandlwana, I have a bone to pick with Madiba. And I love uTata Madiba. He's a cool old man. I especially respect his choice in women. Tata has an eye for them peaches. But he pulled a despicable trick on my pound-for-pound favourite politician of all time, the irascible chief from Ulundi. What a lot people don't realise is that Chief Buthelezi is a direct descendant of King Mpande, Shaka's brother, and that he is possibly one of the world's foremost historical experts on Zulu history. He probably has an acute appreciation of the historical importance of killing people. After all, the great Zulu nation didn't lose power at the Gallagher Estate. I guarantee that if the Chief had been in charge at any stage in the last few years my breakfast wouldn't be spoiled every day by the ordinarily lovely Leanne Cross going on about "The crisis in Zimbabwe". I believe that those R30-billion Rooivalks would have long circled over Harare just daring any mutinous punks to crawl out of their hiding holes. Besides, I suspect that the Chief, with his acute appreciation for history, has a bone to grind with Mzilikazi's offspring scattered all over Zimbabwe. Mzilikazi never brought back the Zulus' cattle that he left with when he headed north. And we Zulus take that sort of thing very seriously.

Point being that I'm sure Tata Madiba was acutely aware of the Chief's war-mongering personality trait. In any case, when some uprising was brewing among our horse-loving neighbours in Lesotho in 1998, Madiba was concerned. He wanted to quell the trouble and nip it the bud without dirtying his own hands. You know, he had to look after his whole poster-boy-for-harmony Nobel Peace laureate image. He looked at his cabinet and didn't like what he saw. If he left it to Mbeki the mutiny would spread all the way to Bloem while Thabo sat there, pipe dangling from lips, posting, "I am an African. I owe my being to hills and koppies of Thaba Bosiu…" on the ANC Today website. So he let the only man who wouldn't hesitate have a go. Yep, the Chief. Shame on you, Tata.

Oh how I would have loved to have been a fly on the wall of that office at the Union Buildings.

Joe Modise: Hi Shenge. What can I do for you?
Chief Buthelezi: Hi Joe. This is your president-for-the-day calling. Please be so kind as to send about 10,000 troops to Maseru right at this moment.
JM: I don't understand. What is our quarrel with the horse people?
CB: Oh, I don't know. Just shoot a few hundred Basotho and their horses, and we'll figure out an explanation when Madiba returns. Your cooperation is much appreciated.

This is the kind of unwavering ballsy action that only someone with Shenge's appreciation for the tradition of killing people would take. Shoot first and apologise later if there are "innocent" bystanders. Although, to evoke again our friend from *Unforgiven*, perhaps we all have it coming. Herewith, another enlightening quote from that fine flick:

Strawberry Alice: You just kicked the shit out of an innocent man.
Little Bill: Innocent? Innocent of what?

I think people like Julius and me are dangerous people. We see the world the way it is: a great big murderous killing field. That's because we have an acute appreciation for history and how killing people is just how things are done. After all, Julius's second-highest grade in his Matric certificate was for History, the subject that chronicles who killed whom (never mind that it was standard-grade D). Perhaps that's our limitation right there. Perhaps we lack the imagination to see the world for what it could be, like Barack Obama. Although I suspect that when Julius Malema becomes the Minister of Education in 2014, you and I will fork out a couple of million for his "VIP Protection", otherwise known as "burly guys with guns prepared to kill people for Julius Malema".

Speaking of Obama, the next four years will surely be interesting to watch. I cannot recall a Commander-in-Chief of the US Armed Forces who didn't issue the "kill" order on a grand scale at least once during his presidency. That includes a sedate peaceful dude like Jimmy Carter. Of course they all call it the "deployment of troops" – except George "Walker Texas Ranger" Bush who calls it "smokin' 'em out of their holes". Will Obama pull a Madiba when Iran inevitably steps out of line (read: tells Obama to stick it up where only the double-ply goes)? Will he plan a sudden trip to his ancestral land, Kenya, and leave Hillary to send in the cruise missiles? After all, you can't be all about change and hope and "Yes we can!" – and then order a multitude of deaths.

But then again, who wouldn't kill for Barack Obama?

Come Off It! You'd Kill For Julius Malema…

Is It Coz I'm Black?

With This Gall Bladder, I Thee Wed

The only time I ever saw my father weep was at my traditional wedding. They were tears of joy. I wanted to weep too. But mine would have been tears of pain. Any married man reading this and not nodding in agreement with me is clearly not an African who got married the traditional way. Allow me to explain.

When it comes right down to it, I truly believe that human beings are essentially the same wherever you go. The factors that drive human behaviour are universal because they are hard-wired into the nucleotide sequence of our DNA. You might read this and shake your head in violent disagreement. After all, you would probably prefer to believe that you aren't driven by the same instincts that motivate Joshua, the shepherd from Otorohanga in New Zealand, who has been known to make amorous advances on the more aesthetically pleasing members of his flock. But that's hardly my point.

My point is that human beings operate at a much more primal level than we like to acknowledge. This fact is especially difficult to acknowledge if you consider yourself a sophisticated member of society. Living in a golf estate in the vicinity of the Tsitsikamma Forest has a way of festering delusions about what truly drives one's actions. In the end, most of what we do is driven by the uncontrollable need to eat, keep warm or cool, take a crap and make babies. Everything else is just detail. Just a part of the unavoidable clutter we like to call life.

I wonder just how many married people have ever taken the time to honestly interrogate the reasons why they got married. What is the source of the insurmountable urge to seek a partner with whom to engage in holy matrimony? A few decades ago, during my grandfather's lifetime, men used to get married for the express purpose of legally partaking in regular sex. That's because back in 1937, females didn't just "put out" willy-nilly. You had to marry them first. Let's all agree that this was a primitive way of living. But by the time I personally entered the reproductive section of the population, females didn't have such Dark Age hang-ups. All a man needed to get regular "play" was a decent pad and a set of wheels and – voilà! – he was in business. Men of my generation from most walks of life would agree with this assessment. (Of course Faizl from Kabul in Afghanistan probably has a slightly different experience. The Taliban was running a tight anti-penetration ship before those democracy evangelists from Hollywood came around.)

It therefore boggles the mind how it came to pass that I found myself walking down the aisle in new toe-pinching pointy shoes next to my bride a few years ago. Before that moment, I had a really good thing going. I can't even pinpoint the moment that I surrendered my freedom; I just never saw it coming. What's even worse is that not one of the Judases who call themselves my friends pointed out to me that I was on this slippery slope until it was too late. The bastards sold me out for a measly 30 slices of the juicy lamb handed to them by my would-be captor every time they came to my place. One minute I'm having a ball enjoying the freedom of my bachelorhood, the next moment I'm having a riveting discussion about floral arrangements with a wedding coordinator.

I have a confession to make. When I said that human beings are the same everywhere, I might have fibbed a little bit. What I meant to say is that human beings are the same *99 per cent of the time*. Allow me to tell you why.

I am an African. That's a much bigger deal than you might think. I do not know what this means to anyone else, but it sure has a lot of significance where weddings are concerned. Intelligent, learned scholars have spent inordinate amounts of brain power and energy trying to answer an important question. How did it come about that an entire continent was captured so easily and colonised? Come now; we've all seen pictures of Jan van Riebeeck. This was no great conqueror in the mould of Genghis Khan. Van Riebeeck was a girly hippie with a curly moustache. How difficult could it have been to rip out his Adam's apple with a bow and arrow? I'll tell you how. I think Africa was so easily colonised because every time the palefaces from Europe paddled onto our shores, we were having one of our three-week-long weddings.

My African brothers know what I'm talking about here. A typical story about a wedding in Paris, say, goes something like this. Boy meets girl in

With This Gall Bladder, I Thee Wed

January. They shack up by February. Boy buys girl an engagement ring and proposes. Girl buys a pretty frock; boy hires a tux. Boy and girl invite 20 of their best friends to their June wedding and say "I do". Fathers-in-law get inebriated and make speeches in which they question the depth of their in-laws' gene pools. Boy and girl go on a honeymoon to the Fiji islands, come back with killer tans and live miserably ever after or until divorce does them part. Whichever one comes first. It's a beautiful thing – enough to make a man cry. Possibly.

In Africa we do things a little differently. For starters, there is the small matter of the transfer of wealth from the future groom to the future bride's family. Back in the day, this wealth transfer was in the form of cattle. Nowadays hard cash is king. Thank God I don't live in Zimbabwe. In these parts this practice is called *ilobolo*, or *magadi* in SeSotho. Intellectual African traditionalist types explain that this custom was designed as a symbol of two families becoming one. The real reason, of course, is that the bride-to-be's family had a sharp understanding that the groom was so desperate for regular spasms he was willing to part with a large herd of bovines.

> *Father of the Wannabe Groom:* Son, this is crazy. I cannot part with 250 head of cattle on account of just one woman.
> *Wannabe Groom:* With all due respect father, I need relief without manual intervention. I'm 25, ferchrissakes!
> *FWG:* Yikes, son! No need to get so graphic now. Here, take 300, just in case.

And this is how it came to pass that I found myself in the parking lot of the Morningside Holiday Inn counting a few hundred R100 bills on the bonnet of an uncle's car one Saturday morning. The absurdity of walking around with that much cash on my person was not lost on me. But the preposterous nature of this scene was completely lost on my uncle, who had flown in from Durban the previous evening. Since the rinderpest outbreak circa 1897, people from my neck of the woods have increasingly been conducting this transaction in hard currency. Of course, what nobody seems to take into consideration is the fact that a perfectly healthy bride, complete with strong teeth and wide child-bearing hips, would probably set one back a couple of shillings back in 1897. The head of one's lobolo delegation could carry this amount in the small pouch covering his groin underneath his *umutsha* – the tails that hang down the front in Zulu traditional garb – even if it was in small bills.

But the 21st-century version of lobolo has transformed from being a somewhat sensible transaction into a neat way for the bride's family to plug the gaping holes in the family coffers opened up by Tito Mboweni's overzealous inflation-targeting interest-rate hikes. Nowadays it is not uncommon for the asking price to be in the region of R50,000. Imagine carrying around that much cash in R20 bills because your branch ran out of higher denominations. And this is not taking into consideration the general messiness of the actual negotiations themselves. Especially if the head of the bridal delegation is a distant illiterate alcoholic uncle who is there on the sole basis of his seniority in the extended family. I have a friend who tells of his head-of-delegation uncle almost suffering a diabetic stroke when a drunk uncle on the other side got his zeros muddled up and asked for R30-million by mistake.

If you're lucky and the whole lobolo wife-for-cash barter thingy goes well, you're now set for the uphill struggle with your respective folks. Back in the day when one was restricted to choosing a wife from one's village or a neighbouring village ten kilometres away, there were a few more steps in the process before the actual wedding day. And each step was always naturally punctuated with the slitting of a medium-sized mammal's throat. For the ancestors, you see. Apparently our ancestors have nothing better to do in the life hereafter than to get boners every time a goat bleats its way to death. I personally think that these intermediary steps before a wedding were historically just an excuse for people to enjoy fresh meat. No freezers and all of that in the 1400s.

And so the groom-to-be's family would visit the bride-to-be's family to hand over gifts. A few weeks later the bride-to-be's family would return the favour and visit the groom-to-be's family, also bearing gifts. It never seemed to occur to anybody that the gifts might be cancelling each other out. Or that you could achieve the same net effect by both sides just staying put at home. Too much fun was being had by all concerned as the beer flowed and the goats tumbled. Of course, even in this day of perfectly functioning double-door Kelvinator ice-boxes, parents insist that this whole goat massacre must continue unabated. I think they just like upsetting the bunny-huggers over at the SPCA.

In my case, I managed to strike a compromise by pointing out that my own future wife's family lived 650 kilometres away in a place called Tshwane. "Tshwane" just sounds much farther away than "Pretoria" when you're in KwaZulu-Natal. The compromise proposal was this: the day before the actual wedding we would all congregate under one roof to exchange gifts, wantonly behead goats and leave the ancestors in a state of general heightened arousal.

Negotiating the next step was a tad trickier. The majority of us Africans in these parts are Christians even as we continue holding on to our African customs. It's not an easy duality to straddle, I tell you. It is for this reason that most of us end up having two parts to our weddings: the white wedding and the traditional wedding. In my case, it was agreed that the white wedding would be in my wife's backyard in Gauteng and the traditional wedding would take place at my folks' place in the Valley of a Thousand Hills. That's correct: home and away fixtures, just like in the Champions League. Hectic stuff, I know. Before you even get to the home-and-away mojo, the bill for this thing is already approaching 50 grand. But who's counting when the ancestors are having such a ball? Like women all over the globe, the African woman has also been dreaming of her special day since her sexist mother gave her her first Borbie doll (the Fong Kong "made in China" version, not to be confused with a genuine Barbie). For women, the whole marriage deal is really all about *THE BIG DAY*. You know, her being a queen for a day as she walks down the aisle with all her friends oohing and aahing over the sheer brilliance of her colour scheme. That whole potentially 60-year-long period after the wedding day is just part of the minor details surrounding *THE BIG DAY*. I would hazard a bet that this is a phone conversation had by many grooms and brides on the morning of their wedding day:

Groom: Baby, I'm sorry but I just can't go through with this.
Bride: Listen here, boet. My dress is perfect, the flowers are awesome and the caterers have already delivered the food.
Groom: But, baby, you don't understand. I've been diddling your sister all this time and we want to be together.
Bride: Insignificant detail. I've been planning this all my life! We *are* having this wedding today! We can annul first thing Monday and you can run off with that little tramp if you must…

On a personal level, making the acute realisation that the wedding day had nothing to do with me saved me a lot of headaches. My job was to put on my "I'm attentive but not meddlesome" face every time a "discussion" about décor, colour themes, menus and suchlike came up. I call it a "discussion" because the discussions had a decidedly undemocratic hijacker-tells-victim-to-lie-down feel about them. I was getting really strong hints that the only acceptable response to everything was "Uh-huh". It was a great move on my part. Blood spillage was kept to the barest minimum. I have known females who chose colour schemes for no other rational reason than to make the groom look ridiculous. My wife was kind enough to allow my groomsmen and me to wear black. Huge sigh of relief. I've seen grooms walk down the aisle looking like human lemon meringues.

As a reward for my general good behaviour (read: staying out of her way), I was also fortunate that I didn't have to go to a hair salon and get a fancy hairdo. On my wedding day, I looked mostly like me if you ignore the fact that I was washed and shaven, and smelled like a toiletry bag. This is a rarity for me on a Saturday morning. Still, I got off easy. I have a friend who got married in the early '90s. His bride insisted that he went the S-curl-and-cut route. You'll recognise it as that greasy hairdo favoured by African-American TV evangelists and other generally oily holy men of the calibre of the Honourable Reverend Meshoe.

The S-curl went out of favour a couple of decades back, though some prominent black men such as Romeo Khumalo and Robert Marawa have been admirably holding the fort down the years. And I'm not judging them by any means. Each man to his shiny own. But I *am* judging my friend's wife for insisting on taking out their wedding album each time I visit. And there he'll be, S-curl glistening in the sun as if someone hit him over the head with a bottle of cooking oil. The oily creature on the crown of his head looks like it would put on a blue overall, white gumboots and burst into a rendition of "Shosholoza" if you tossed a few coins in its direction.

Moving on from the ridiculous appearance of the poor, hapless groom, then there's the ceremony itself, with obligatory fanfare, lengthy sermons and way too much ululating from Aunty Jumaima, no doubt helped along by the nip of Smirnoff inside her handbag. Everybody has an Aunty Jumaima.

This is always followed by that whole baffling practice where the bride and groom drive to some scenic botanical garden two hours away for photographs. The long and short of this is that parched and famished guests loiter around the reception hall, melting in 450°C heat, emptying flower vases to drink the water and nibbling on the R500-a-bunch floral arrangements for sustenance. This is why I have learnt never to attend an African wedding without grabbing some chicken wings on my way there and bringing my cooler box with "goodies". By the time the reception commences, five hours later, all the diabetics in the hall have lapsed into hypoglycaemic coma from lack of food. This is one of the few things I insisted on for my wedding. To avoid anybody passing out on our account, we went straight to lunch after the ceremony. After all, most people attend weddings for food, booze and the chance to meet the multitudes of desperate singles.

Then, of course, it's time for the long-winded verbose speeches from every relative who ever changed your diaper when you were two months old. Followed shortly thereafter by the battle of the titans. Yep, the father-of-the-bride (FOB) trying to outdo the father-of-the-groom (FOG) with the best speech of the day. Whenever I'm asked about the outcome at my own wedding I always give the politically correct answer: it was a tie. This is often the most entertaining part of the whole thing for me when I attend weddings. Due to a combination of the heat, dehydration and too much booze, it is not unheard of for the FOB to stand at the podium and let everybody know that his in-laws never paid the lobolo in full. I rate such moments as the best fun money can't buy. Especially if someone instructs the deejay to drown him out with music and the senile ol' FOB continues shouting in any case. If the bride breaks down in tears as a result, I snap away with the camera. And should the groom follow suit, I get the urge to randomly throw small bills towards them like I'm at Teazers.

Some couples don't stop there with the good stuff. They actually hire those amateur a cappella quartets who will predictably attempt a Boyz II Men classic at some point. All because one of them is Aunty Jumaima's son whose claim to fame is that he was knocked out in round one of the *Idols* auditions but managed to appear on TV in the process. Now you have four tone-deaf bleating goats on stage murdering a Motown classic so badly Marvin Gaye is turning in his grave. It's all in the spirit of good fun if you're a spectator. But if you're the groom, you have that deep faraway look often seen on the faces of guilty defendants as the verdict is being read out. That's because you're contemplating the second half of this torture: the traditional wedding. In my own case, the torture was planned for the Saturday following the white wedding.

I have no idea how African traditional weddings used to go, say, 500 years ago. I imagine that they were orderly affairs where everybody knew the protocol and all the role players knew their parts. It is with a heavy heart that I have to report that the 21st-century version of the same event has as much order and direction as a class of four-year-olds with attention deficit disorder who've just had a sugar fix. And no amount of prior planning can help you out. Your first problem will always boil down to our African obsession with separating the body and soul of mammals. And

With This Gall Bladder, I Thee Wed

for the main event it's the big mammals made popular by McDonald's. To slaughter one, two or 17, that is the question. Depends on how much of a frenzy one wants to whip the ancestors into, I guess. In my case, after an exhausting exercise in circular logic, out of sheer exasperation I finally agreed on two.

And then, of course, the gangster mentality associated with traditional weddings kicks in. Which beast will be consumed by which side? Asking such clearly ill-informed questions always results in the elders shaking their heads and making the sign of the cross. (What happened to *ilobolo* making us all one big happy family?) So you bite your tongue and watch this runaway train hurtle towards its natural conclusion. And then there's a discussion about the fact that the bridal party must dispatch their own beast and the groom's family their own. And then when the departure of the beasts' souls has been expedited, the carcasses must be split down the middle and halves swapped. Just in case the bride's family want to poison the groom's family I guess. Not even the 26s and the 28s at Pollsmoor Prison have such little faith in the goodwill of the other gang…

Next thing, the bridal party finds itself standing on one side of the yard with the groom's family on the other in a face-off reminiscent of the Springboks staring down an All Blacks haka before a test match. But it's not a haka forthcoming; it's a sing-off, the objective of which is to drown the other side out with your impressive vocal chords. For a visual, just think Michael Jackson's "Beat It" video minus the knives. Although there will, of course, be knobkerries and shields. On my special day it wasn't even a contest; it was a lopsided massacre. Zulu vocal chords from the Valley are legendary in their magnitude and pitch.

This warlike situation will always culminate in the climax of the whole day, when the groom is made to lie on a mat or bed and the women from the bridal party are encouraged to donner him to a pulp. I'm not making this up.

After all of that, the bride is still not a member of the groom's family. That's correct; two cows dead, carcass halves exchanged, the bride's family shouted down and the groom assaulted, not to mention an entire religious wedding the week before – but no, she is still not a member of the family. Amidst all the blood-letting of the large mammals, there is the small matter of the ancestors' favourite medium-sized mammal which also needs to expire. Only when the bride is smeared with bile from the goat's gall bladder are you truly engaged in matrimony in the eyes of the ancestors. And they are pleased.

Six months after my wedding, my bank balance was still minus R50,000. I walked around muttering unintelligible things to myself like a hobo. I was given to regular involuntary facial twitches. I had to endure nightmares about headless goats chasing me around, bleating Boyz II Men's "End Of The Road" through their bloodied gullets. It's only when I woke up and looked at my sleeping bride that I would think to myself, "You know, it was worth all the fuss."

Is It Coz I'm Black?

The Afrikaner-Americans Of The East Rand

Until I started working and living in the East Rand towns of Boksburg and Benoni a little less than a decade ago, I was not too *au fait* with the ways of the Afrikaner.

One of the anomalies of growing up in and around the (then) Natal coastal city of Durban is that I never interacted much with any Afrikaans-speaking people. The only white people I got to see regularly were prim-and-proper Englishmen with stiff upper lips. They lived in the leafy suburbs of Hillcrest, Kloof and Waterfall, and I would typically see them during my mom's weekly shopping sojourn into Pinetown, with my knuckleheaded self in tow.

My first memory of an Afrikaner is a farmer who peddled curdled milk from the back of his Chevrolet bakkie in my Mpumalanga Township Unit 1 North neighbourhood west of Durban. He had flame-coloured hair, a beetroot-like complexion from overexposure to the sun and rough, calloused, soil-tilling mini parachutes for hands. He would stand in the back of his bakkie next to stainless-steel canisters of maas, a fermented milk staple, yelling, *"Makhafula nank' amasi!"* [Kaffirs, I bring you maas!], into a loud-hailer to alert residents that the sour-milk trader had arrived.

I guess that if you are uninitiated in the mood of my obscure corner of the world, circa 1975, you are probably wondering how people took to being called kaffirs. The truth is there wasn't much of a reaction other than a few mumblings along the lines of, *"Kodwa kwenzenjani leliBhunu lisibiza ngamakhafula nje?"* [But is it really necessary for this Boer to call us kaffirs?], as people shoved coins into his outstretched parachutes in exchange for their fermented delights. In the mid-'70s, Mpumalanga Township Unit 1 North was unlike the other politically militant Durban townships of Clermont, KwaMashu or Lamontville. The extent of any political activity in my neighbourhood was a bunch of women in tight-fitting khaki uniforms singing catchy tunes about the saintly halo around the head of one Chief Mangosuthu Buthelezi and his general Messiah tendencies. Most of the songs were heavily borrowed from Methodist hymn books, of course.

In any case, I think that anyone offended by the kaffir characterisation would have been dissuaded from taking a moral stand by the double-barrelled shotgun and cattle whip that the curdled-milk dispenser always kept ominously in sight. Nothing like the threat of one's brain splattered all over the tarmac to sharpen that pragmatism. Or a whip cracking on one's skin. Besides, the local primary school principal, Mr Msimang, was married to a coloured woman who used the word *ikhafula*, the Zulu corruption of kaffir, quite liberally to berate the Cele boys every time they raided her orchard and left a trail of dusty footprints in her garden. If anybody had a problem with being called *ikhafula*, they would have to deal with Mrs Msimang. Physically. Mr Cele, father to the peach-redistribution technicians, found this out when he took issue with her over the kaffirisation of his boys. As Mrs Msimang sat on his chest, her fleshy thighs around his ears, pummelling his drunken face with her fists, Mr Cele – and I suspect most of the men in the neighbourhood – decided that it was probably smarter to just live and let live. Who cared what some Boesman woman with pumpkin-coloured skin called you? Especially when she was clearly a long-lost cousin of Muhammad Ali.

The Afrikaners come from a long line of great and heroic people, going back all the way to the Dutch sailors who docked at the Cape of Good Hope on the 6th of April in the 1,652nd year of our Lord. Each time I read about the shenanigans of those early Dutch settlers, I so wish I had a photograph of the occupants of the *Drommedaris* as they stepped ashore. This is the type of situation that requires a visual, and I would pay a lot of money to have just one pictorial depiction of that moment. But I suspect that the 17th-century *Khoi Gazette* photographer was covering another event when the ship rolled into Table Bay. I imagine that the members of the village welcoming committee were probably at the same event. I'm thinking a traditional wedding myself. But what I would really have loved to see is the look on their faces as they disembarked from the *Drommedaris*. Based on the events that followed their arrival, I imagine they must have been quite peckish for some biltong because the transfer of cattle ownership between them and the locals was to dominate most of the news in the decades to follow (and must have featured prominently in the *Khoi Gazette* – probably as frequently as the marital trials and tribulations of Steve Hofmeyr feature in *Beeld* today). I imagine they must have been quite horny, too. If the subsequent general complexion of the Western Cape is anything to go by, then I'm probably right.

In the years, decades and centuries that followed, the Afrikaner people spawned some of the greatest heroes this part of the world has ever seen. I'm talking about Piet Retief, Hendrick Potgieter, Christian de Wet and Paul Kruger, to name a few. Paul Kruger alone had more courage-juice in the impressive bags under his eyes than an entire DRC-based battalion during Mosiuoa Lekota's unimpressive tenure at the helm of the Ministry of Defence. But what about the average Afrikaner?

A few years ago I spent an evening in a pool bar on Brakpan's notorious Voortrekker Street in the company of a one-eyed fellow called Krapies. This particular Voortrekker Street is not to be confused with the other Voortrekker Streets in Springs, Benoni, Boksburg, Kempton Park, Roodepoort, Ladybrand, Bloemfontein, Pofadder and other such impressive places. This was Voortrekker Street in Brakpan.

I had stopped at this bar inside a "hotel" to get some after-hours beer replenishment when Krapies approached me to implore me to contribute generously to his beer fund. Before I knew it, Krapies was regaling me with colourful stories of Boer heroism going back to the Cape Colony days under Simon van der Stel's watchful eye. I'm a sucker for great war stories, so I kept him fed with a steady supply of Carling Black Labels served in Brakpan pints – you know, those 750ml ones. Krapies's recollection got clearer and his descriptions more vivid with each "pint". By the end of the evening I discovered that Krapies had lost his eye at the Battle of Majuba while fighting alongside Paul Kruger during the first Anglo-Boer War. My crude arithmetic revealed to me that I was having a conversation with a 163-year old living legend. To say I was amazed is an understatement. Krapies didn't look much older than 50, judging by his jet-black slicked-backed hair. I made a mental note to go on a bobotie, kudu biltong and Black Label diet from that day on.

My favourite Krapies story involved the great Paul Kruger himself. Apparently Kruger and a small band of not more than 15 men had left camp on horseback to go searching for firewood during the Boer War when they found themselves surrounded by an entire British regiment. All the men panicked except for Kruger. That's because a voice suddenly started to speak to him, issuing him with instructions on what to do. The voice emanated from a flame-engulfed baobab tree stump that did not burn out. So while a furious battle ensued between his few good men and the British regiment, Kruger sat still on his horse, his pipe raised to the heavens. According to the voice, as long as his pipe was raised, his men would not be vanquished. And it was so. I had had quite a few Brakpan pints of the golden nectar of the gods myself by this stage of the storytelling, but I could swear I vaguely remembered reading a similar tale in some thick book with tiny print. But Krapies insisted that the story was true and that there is even a rock monument commemorating this very event on the western slope of Proclamation Hill at the Voortrekker Monument. If I didn't believe him, why not take a drive there? I declined the invitation and bade him an emotional farewell. I prefer to keep my excursions to the Voortrekker Monument to a bare minimum, especially around mid-December. I like to avoid messy misunderstandings such as those sometimes experienced by speedy dark-hued rugby winger Jongi Nokwe at Loftus Versfeld. You can call me a yellow-bellied poor excuse for a Zulu warrior if you want; I'm cool with that.

This is the colourful character of the place-formerly-known-as-the-East-Rand these days. You don't publicly call it Ekurhuleni, of course, unless you're willing to step outside and physically explain what you mean. Often, I drive around the suburbs of Ekurhuleni and I wonder what those great founding fathers of Afrikanerdom would feel about the 2008 Boksburg version of the fruit of their loins. Would they approve or would they violently shake their impressive beards in disappointment? What would they think of the rows of houses with sprawling neatly manicured lawns in the suburb of Sunward Park? I imagine they'd be quite impressed with the proliferation of those entertainment areas with thatched roofs called lapas. I imagine that the smell of boerewors and T-bone throughout Els Park every Saturday afternoon would find resonance within Piet Retief if he woke up from the grave. I think he'd stroke his beard and feel that the Great Trek was not another wasted Amazing Race-type exercise on ox wagons, after all.

But I have to wonder how he'd feel about some of the more disturbing aspects of life in Ekurhuleni. You see, if you took someone from America's Midwest and planted them in the middle of Benoni, they'd be forgiven for thinking they were back in Deer Creek, Oklahoma.

When I first moved to Ekurhuleni, light was shed on a mystery that had always bugged me. I knew that the Ford Motor Company operated in South Africa. I had seen a few Ford dealerships back in Durban. And I had seen the Ford Fiesta ads on TV. But where things got a little hazy for me was in answer to the question, "Who drives Fords?" And even more importantly, "Where did all those Fords from the '70s and '80s go?" There certainly weren't that many Fords anywhere else I'd ever been before. The mystery was solved the first week I lived in Benoni, when I encountered every model of Ford imaginable: Ford Escorts, Ford Granadas, Ford Sierra XR6s, Ford Sapphire Ghias, and even their cousin, the Chevrolet El Camino. All in shiny, pristine condition, and with wide sparkling mag wheels.

If you, too, have been wondering where all the Ford Cortinas went, wonder no more. Just come to Benoni town on a Friday evening and you'll find them parked outside one of the 200 or so roadhouses sprinkled all over the East Rand. No, your eyes are not playing tricks on you. Roadhouses. You've seen them in those low-budget Hollywood B-grade flicks with a road-trip theme, featuring used-to-be-stars like Burt Reynolds or Patrick Swayze. You drive in, sit in your car and order your greasy Dagwood/pork-rib/slap-chip combo from a cardboard menu brought to you by a young lady who looks like she used to work the corner of Empire and Claim in her former life. And to complete the Midwest theme, they're all named the Mississippi Grill, the Dallas Burger Ranch or the Alabama Burger Palace.

If that doesn't convince you of the American connection, then I invite you to come out to the Springs Burger Centrum on a month-end non-Currie Cup Saturday evening. Certainly not a Saturday involving the Bulls in any case. You'll see the same Ford Cortinas parked outside the civic centre hall with a Wild West saloon-bar theme. Strange-looking men in checked shirts, Lee denim jeans and veldskoene will emerge from the Ford-convention parking lot. They will have Brylcreemed hair, short on the sides with sideburns and a wavy tuft of hair at the back. Yep, the mullet never left the East Rand. Long after Karl Kikillus stopped playing that Achy Breaky guy's song on *Pop Shop*. Of course it didn't help matters that each time I flipped through *Huisgenoot* Steve Hofmeyr was staring back at me with those blue eyes in the centre spread. And Steve hung in there with his own version of the Achy Breaky mullet well into the '90s...

But back to the Springs Burger Centrum hall. Blaring inside the hall will be a bizarre type of music: a mix between country-and-western, folk and boeremusiek. The performers will be artists no-one living west of the East Rand Mall has ever heard of. I'm talking about okes called Pieter Koen and Kurt Darren. If you said "Kurt who?", you clearly need to get some much-needed culture into your one-dimensional life. Believe me, Kurt Darren is *HUGE* in Geduld, Krugersrus and the rest of Bokkieland. This is the guy who rocked Springs throughout the summer of 2008/9. But if you want something a little bit mellow on a Sunday afternoon, then I suggest that you pop into the Brakpan Civic Centre hall for straight-up country music, with the headline act being one Bobby Angel. I know. Most people think Bobby Angel died the same year that Jock from Dallas died. No, he didn't. He performs in Brakpan every Sunday. And if you do not know who Bobby Angel is then I guess you were not around to watch *Gentle On My Mind* on Sunday afternoons back in 1981 when we only had one TV channel.

As I go around the East Rand taking all of this in, I continue wondering just what the great Paul Kruger would feel about his kleinkinders. How would he feel about the fact that Brakpan's greatest export in the entire 20th century was Mike Schutte, the former boxer who was the subject of

The Afrikaner-Americans Of The East Rand 73

the Mike Schutte jokes that rendered Van der Merwe jokes obsolete? But more importantly, what would President Kruger say when told that the most senior Afrikaner politician in the land is a Trompie-lookalike most people insist on calling Kortbroek? That the name of the great General de Wet is nowadays only being shouted in obscure Boksburg Noord halls during meetings convened by a fiery demagogue best known for a mishap while performing an equestrian trick?

The reason I first came to live in Ekurhuleni was to join the R&D department of a large multinational corporation as a product-and-process developer at one of its food-processing plants. My role included helping our third-party partner factories with their processing. It was at one of these plants that I met a man who helped me shape my perspective on Afrikaners. Well into his sixties, he was (and still is) the factory manager of his plant, known to the men and women he managed simply as Kwaaibaas, or Angry Boss. Our tumultuous working relationship did not have the greatest of beginnings at all. As a matter of fact, I had already concluded that he was a rabid AWB-supporting racist within ten minutes of meeting him. It didn't help matters any that the first words he ever uttered to me were, "Morning, young man. I am Mr Piet Geldenhuys" – not really his name – "but everybody calls me Kwaaibaas." Things went from bad to worse when he kept on referring to everybody as "that black lady" or "this black man". And maybe that does make him an old racist bastard. But that type of thing has never fazed me too much. The overwhelming majority of people I know are racist swine anyway.

I became truly fascinated by old Kwaaibaas the first time we sat down together outside of our work environment. It was the last Friday of the working year, in December. We had just successfully hit the annual production tonnage quota, which meant I had hit my personal target. So we went out for a drink in a Boksburg pub. Since he was having a Klippies-and-Coke I thought to myself, why not also have a Klippies-and-Coke, the spiritual drink of Boksburg? This was the first time I'd been introduced to the unique buzz that one can only experience from Klippies. You could say it was something of a life milestone. The first thing I noticed was that

I developed a sudden craving for dried meat, or biltong, if you will. Next thing I knew I was peppering my speech with expletives, even though we were having a very cordial conversation. Everything was "fokken this" and "fokken that". Where I got seriously concerned was when I got up to empty the Klippies tank in the bathroom and found myself humming "Sarie Marais" under my breath. And the transformation was complete when I started getting uncontrollable urges to donner a kaffir for no reason… But of course I jest. And I digress.

That Friday afternoon Kwaaibaas said some things to me that made me think. He told me of the number of times that he had been hauled in front of one or other disciplinary hearing to answer racism charges against him. This had occurred a few years earlier while he was employed by a large multinational beverage manufacturer as a production supervisor. And this is what had led to him being retrenched from that job in the early '90s after 30-odd years of service. I was sitting there thinking, "Here we go again, I'm about to hear all about the evils of affirmative action and how since the black man has taken over there is no future for the white man, and all that tired crap about reverse racism and so forth." Yawn.

But he surprised me when he said, "Of course they were right to fire me. I had it coming."

Huh?

Kwaaibaas went on to explain to me how he had grown up in a little farming town in the northern Free State in the middle of nowhere. He talked about how, growing up, everybody just "knew" and accepted that black people were a little slow and perhaps even a lower form of humanity. How he honestly did not know that the word "kaffir" was a bad or hurtful word. How the black farm labourers of his town seemed to be accepting of this situation and seemed quite happy with their lot in life. The first time the notion ever entered his mind that something was wrong with this situation, he told me, was in the '60s. He was in his mid-twenties working as an artisan in a factory. The black workers had downed tools and were protesting. His story reminded me of a "joke" that had been doing the email circuit in the late '90s:

The Afrikaner-Americans Of The East Rand   75

A Brakpan local had been involved in an accident involving a black pedestrian and was in court explaining his side of the story.

"En toe ek om die draai kom, sien ek 'n kaffir…" [And when I came around the bend, I saw a kaffir…]

The judge bangs the table with his gavel and interjects:

"Meneer, ek sal nie daardie taalgebruik in my hof toelaat nie." [Sir, I won't allow that kind of language in my court.]

The Brakpan ou gives the judge a confused look and begins again:

"En toe ek om die draai kom, sien ek 'n kaffir…" [And when I came around the bend, I saw a kaffir…]

"Meneer Strydom! Ek waarsku u vir die laaste keer! Moenie kaffir se nie. Se 'n swart man." [Mr Strydom! I'm warning you for the last time. Do not say a kaffir. Say a black man.]

"Goed dan. En toe ek om die draai kom, sien ek 'n… 'n swart man… Ai, maar edel agbare, ek is seker dit was 'n kaffir wat ek gesien het." [Okay then. And when I came around the bend, I saw a… a black man… Hey, but Your Lordship, I'm pretty certain I saw a kaffir.]

So I sat there listening to Kwaaibaas speaking to me very openly, but without any of that false apologetic bullshit that people tend to put on when they talk about these things. The reason Afrikaners tended to get tagged with the racism label, he offered, is not so much that they are necessarily more racist than anyone else. Rather, he explained, the boere are just too blunt for their own good. They lacked the sophistication to package their brand of racism subtly like the British did when they were in charge.

Maybe it's because I was full of Klippies-and-Coke, but what he said made a lot of sense to me at the time. What resonated with me most about our little dop session is when he shrugged and said, "Maybe we Afrikaners seem like we're more hard-headed because we care so much about this place. What everybody forgets is that for us this is the only home we have. Perhaps this is why we're so passionate that things must not go wrong.

Because we'll still be here long after the kak hits the fan. Or maybe we're just simple bastards. Ag, I don't know about these complicated political things. Let's have another double."

That's the type of honesty and simple language that appeals to me. A Xhosa friend of mine once told me that Afrikaners and Zulus make for great bedfellows because we're one of a kind. We're equally blunt and unfettered by the need to clutter our lives with unnecessary sophistication. At the time, it sounded like an insult, like he was saying Afrikaners and Zulus are simpletons. But as I sat there sipping on corrosive brandy-and-coke in a Boksburg pub, I had a minor epiphany. I realised that I liked Kwaaibaas and that the reason I liked him is because we share a quality. And that the quality in question is an appreciation for simplicity and bluntness. Perhaps my friend is right and simplicity is an intrinsic quality that Afrikaners and Zulus share. When I sniff at this "fact", there is more than a tiny whiff of BS about it, but I'm not one to argue against conventional wisdoms.

All I know is that I was in the company of an individual who shared this appreciation for simplicity. I liked the fact that we could have such an uncomfortable discussion without the customary cloak-and-dagger crap normally associated with such conversations. I sat there looking at his bloodshot eyes and thick hands and thought, "These hands probably donnered three generations of kaffirs but somehow it's going to be okay in the future."

Simplicity. A major part of why I love the metropolitan city of Ekurhuleni is because of its simplicity. It makes sense to me. There is a certain simplicity I love about characters such as Krapies. There's a certain simplicity about the Ford Granadas congregated at the roadhouse on Tom Jones Avenue in Benoni. There's a certain simplicity about tannies in floral frocks squealing in near-orgasmic delight as Bobby Angel struts his stuff in a Brakpan pub that shares a street with an NG Kerk.

Or maybe I just love this place.

Is It Coz I'm Black?

Honk If You Feel Your Taxes Aren't Working For You

Only a few short millennia ago, our world was a sparsely populated planet. From what we can extrapolate based on available scientific evidence, it seems that humans were organised into isolated groupings that can be loosely called clans, tribes or gangs. A modern example of such a grouping is the 28s gang at Pollsmoor Prison.

Back in the day, we used to pass the time ripping out cactus plants by their roots with our bare hands, devouring the intestines of antelopes we caught on foot, painting our faces green using animal dung and having free-for-all sex orgies afterwards. In short, it was the perfect life. Marriage had not been invented, you see. Decision-making on the planet was an uncomplicated, efficient process. The smartest, most handsome and most sexually attractive members of any tribe would just naturally float to the surface, become king or queen and rule unopposed in perpetuity or until someone better-looking came along.

And this is, you might surmise, how we ended up with impressive monarchs in the mould of King Mswati, King Zwelithini and Prince Charles. Well, in the case of Prince Charles, when the old hag croaks.

Except you have to factor in an evil, possessed gang called the Moors. The Moors were a fearsome tribe who went around bludgeoning anybody they didn't like with blunt axes. For a mental picture, just think of a whole bunch of Shaquille O'Neals and other NBA basketball stars running around on the rampage. You must admit, they had a point. If your tribe consisted of men who all looked like Shaquille O'Neal and you wandered into a place like Italy with human rodents for a population, wouldn't you hack them to death or try to fornicate your superior genes into their midst?

The problem came in a moment of madness while touring Greece, when the Moors thought it'd be a great prank if they taught the Greeks about a system of governance called "democracy" and see what craziness would ensue. For the record, "democracy" is a Moor word passed on to the Greeks which, loosely translated, means "fixing what ain't broke".

For many centuries the plague of democracy was restricted to far-flung places such as central and western Europe and pockets of the Middle East. The Chinese dabbled in this craziness before they saw the sheer folly of it all and created Chairman Mao. This is why China is preparing to take over the world in the next ten years or so. But somewhere in the middle of the 20th century some overzealous European tribes, including one from a small island in the northern Atlantic, started taking the whole thing a bit too seriously and began spreading the democracy foolishness. Apparently the last king of the Moors was on his deathbed when he heard about the madness. His dying words before he departed this world were (in Moorish), *"Hawu, kanti leziziphukuphuku azidlaliswa yini?"*, which is something along the lines of, "Can't these people take a joke?"

And that is how we have ended up with the likes of Terror Lekota, Patricia de Lille and Badih Chaaban in our government. At the risk of repeating myself, democracy sucks. This is not because it is intrinsically flawed. No. Democracy sucks because it relies on the collective wisdom of *everybody* in the population. And that's just preposterous. I mean, who doesn't know that any country's citizens can be loosely divided into two groups made up of five per cent smart knowledgeable people and 95 per cent "others" – that is, morons wading nutsack-deep in a shallow genetic pool? I'm in the 95 per cent section and even *I* know this. Isn't this the reason why we pay Tito Mboweni somewhere in the region of R700,000,000 a year, with a 175 per cent annual increase? Isn't this our way of recognising that we are idiots who can't be trusted with intricate decisions such as convening the CPM and then raising the repo rate by 50 basis points each time the oil prices go up? Yet according to democratic principles, the guy I saw earlier today pissing against the wind and wondering where the spray was coming from has got as much of a democratic voice as Tito the Boffin. "One man, one vote" is serious retardation, clearly.

When the Moors left Greece, the people of that intellectually dubious country formed a government based on democratic principles that they dubbed Athenian democracy. No-one quite knows why they called it that. A Moor queen called Athanasia, perhaps? In any case, in Athenian democracy they had something called the Assembly of the Citizens. This

Honk If You Feel Your Taxes Aren't Working For You

was a congregation of all the male citizens who spent their time debating, calling each others' moms whores, voting about stuff and indulging in other general flatulence-generating activities. Tune into the Parliament channel on DStv for reference. Scholars tell us that this was called direct or participative democracy. And it was not on grounds of sexism that females were excluded. The Assembly apparently always coincided with that part of the lunar cycle when women were inexplicably irrational and prone to wild mood swings. It's the same principle the Vatican has been using to keep women from dispensing His body and His blood during Holy Mass for centuries. Well, that and the fact that afterwards they could all go "Greek" on each other without being judged. Our own Desmond Dube, the actor-turned-activist, used a similar principle when he organised his Million Men March. Why men and not women? As a result, that non-event was mostly attended by about 1,500 Hillbrow Nigerians and a healthy sprinkling of hobos from the general Joubert Park area. But I'm getting sidetracked.

We do not practise Athenian democracy in this country. That is because about 70 per cent of males in this country are black. And everybody knows that 17.5 million black men congregated in one place is not an Assembly but a riot just waiting to unfold. At least that's the view popularised by that famous foot-licker Adriaan Vlok in the '80s and early '90s in any case. Although the marauding mob that calls itself SATAWU has been known to reinforce this view in downtown Cape Town from time to time.

Our democracy is neither direct nor participative for reasons adequately amplified above. Our complex system depends on making that cross on the ballot. And we don't even get to choose the superior individuals we want to lead us. No, we choose from a buffet of street gangs with short acronyms: the DA, the ID, the ANC, the IFP, the UDM, COPE and so on. If we've been inhaling ganja, the holy herb, we may even be known to put our cross next to the PAC or even the ACDP. And then we go home in the safe knowledge that Pheko and the Rev Meshoe have got our backs.

This is the extent of our democratic participation which, we are told, we must defend and be prepared to die for. In April 1994, during the first democratic elections, I almost died defending this right. I estimate that 60 per cent of my brain cells melted as I stood in that queue. By the time I got to the booth I had lost most of my bodily fluids and a mild case of dementia had set in. It took me about 45 minutes before I could tell the difference between Clarence Makwetu and Nelson Mandela. One 81-year-old man was not so lucky. After all of that, he was led away from the polling station sobbing uncontrollably, "They looked so alike, I voted for the wrong one!" The heartless officials would hear none of it and it was left to his geriatric posse to console him by stuffing a lollipop in his mouth. Octogenarians love sweets. And that's how I think the PAC achieved about two per cent of the vote in 1994, double its showing in subsequent elections.

In case anyone is curious, I'm not advocating the return of the monarchy. Kings have a way of sitting on their thrones all day re-arranging the stones inside their scrotal sacs, getting acute attacks of paedophilia and marrying teenagers. We can't have that. Although something can be said about the calibre of monarchs from just a few hundred years ago; I'd take Moshoeshoe, Hintsa, Shaka, Cetshwayo, Sekhukhune or Ngungunyana over Helen Zille or Bantu Holomisa on any given Sunday. It's just a pity about their spawn. So I'll have to begrudgingly admit that we need to scratch the monarchy idea. I'll tell you what I *am* advocating, though, now that democracy and monarchy are out.

Enter oligarchy. For the benefit of the 95 per cent "others" reading this, an oligarchy is a form of government where a few elite (read: the five per cent) get to make all the decisions. The more astute reader is already shaking her head vigorously, thinking, "But isn't a cabinet some form of oligarchy in any case?" If you thought that, then bingo! Within all democratic states there has effectively been an acknowledgement that a fair level of "rule by the elite" is essential. Of course, the reasons advanced are always iffy and, frankly, with more than just a whiff of BS. The reason we have a cabinet with lots of important cabinet ministers is not because having everybody in a democracy rule is impractical. Oh no. The reason we have cabinet ministers is so that an oligarchic anointed few can rule. So far so good.

There's only one problem with the limited oligarchy we're already practising. It is the democratic process that leads up to it. The poor president has to choose from a pool of Members of Parliament, most of whom come from the infected 95 per cent "others" list. I like to refer to a general election as a big shake-up during which some cream rises to the top amidst a whole lot of scum. That is parliament. Some cream and loads of scum with much noisy aplomb but without much functionality. This is the case with our parliament and this is the theme with parliaments everywhere, including the much-vaunted parliaments of Germany, Sweden, the UK, the US and the rest of those revered Western nations. In all these places, the people making the decisions are a varied selection of looters, plunderers, thieves and retards, who would serve humanity best if they were all given scissors and box cutters and left to run around unsupervised through the corridors of power. The ensuing bloodbath would be a great start to solving the problem.

South Africa is no different. Our (pre-2009 elections) Minister of Correctional Services, Ngconde Balfour, is presumably the best candidate for that position. And our current Minister of Thumb-twiddling (otherwise known as Minister in the Presidency), Manto Tshabalala-Msimang, is also ostensibly the best candidate for her position of looking sharp during cabinet meetings while doing exactly diddly-squat. In case you think I'm picking on poor Manto because she's an easy target due to her much-publicised liver-shrinking activities, think again. As a matter of fact, you could take a resident of Sterkfontein Psychiatric Hospital, ply him with two bottles of cheap brandy, blindfold him, give him darts and ask him to hit an efficient minister on a poster of Mbeki's cabinet circa mid-2008. Whether he hit Stofile, Xingwana, Erwin, Mabandla or Sonjica is immaterial. Same difference. And even with the T-boss gone – hey, at least Manto's not Minister of Health any more – it's still the same difference.

I can hear some people responding along the lines of, "Yes, but we do have some competent ministers. Why not write about them?" My reply to that would be to tell you to stop smoking dehydrated goat's dung and talk only when you know what's going on. "Competent" is a word used to describe individuals who are "not quite incompetent". It's a word that describes mediocrity. If my surreal alcohol intake were to make a liver transplant necessary (assuming I had friends in high places who would let me jump the queue), I wouldn't willingly lie on that butcher's block if I was told the surgeon was competent. I'd want the super-intelligent expert in the field of removing my Jack Daniel's-soaked liver and replacing it with the wholesome liver of a Hare Krishna faithful.

And that's why I think that a proper form of oligarchy is the best form of government. Scratch any democratic election to choose members of parliament. The electorate is the bunch of Einsteins who have already sent Marthinus van Schalkwyk, Pieter Mulder and Bhutana Khompela to parliament. That's a big fat F for effing poor effort in my report card. No, what we need is to convene a convention to choose a parliament of elites with all the foremost experts in all fields of governance. With the political will, it could be done. You might not think it, but there is an absolute authority and expert in any discipline.

For instance, wouldn't you want to know who has the best educationalist brain in the land? Surely it cannot be that English woman who's the current minister. I'm personally torn between Ernest Jansen of the University of Johannesburg and Malegapuru Makgoba of the University of KwaZulu-Natal. They seem keen to present themselves as such with their regular public pronouncements in the print and electronic media. The Vice-Chancellor of the University of Free State was in the running until his institution started churning out world-acclaimed food-whizzers of note. I'd personally want Malegapuru to win, if only just to fuck with white people. It's a tad difficult to call 702 and whinge about the minister of education when you can't pronounce his name, isn't it? I suspect that Makgoba is way ahead of me and has given it a lot of thought. That's why he ditched his other name, William.

But can you seriously imagine a cabinet where each minister was the absolute no-quibbles number-one brain in the land in that department? I am absolutely confident that there is such a thing as the best economics brain in this nation. Now, *that's* who I want in charge of the economy. Ditto the best criminologist brain: that's the fellow I want in charge of Safety and Security. Not Charles Nqakula, the guy who pronounces the word "police" as "please". Who are we begging here? Don't *you* want a sage, an expert with scientifically proven methods, running shit? And no, that person is not Nathi Mthethwa.

We wouldn't even make any pretence of considering them servants of the people. Just call them the Council of the Elites and stand up each time they enter the room. This oligarchic system would be like a form of scientific monarchy. Everybody would know that these are a higher form of humanity; persons of substance. To quote again from that fine philosophical film, *Unforgiven*, this time the words of the character English Bob: "It is uncivilised shooting persons of substance… If you were to try to assassinate a king, sir, the, how shall I say it, the aura of royalty would cause you to miss. But, the president, I mean, why not shoot the president?" Can you imagine anyone calling His Majesty the King Zwelithini "a dog"? But Mbhazima Shilowa – well, why not call Shilowa a dog? You must admit that this logic is watertight.

Sadly, as passionate as I am about this, it would never happen. That's because we have an electorate that despises superior human beings. The electorate wants "men and women of the people". In other words, we want to be led by people who are neither dumber nor smarter than we are. Whether they admit it or not, the hordes who removed Thabo Mbeki from office were informed to a large extent by this phenomenon. A lot was said about his haughty ways. I personally prefer my presidents arrogant, elitist and absolutely convinced that they are super-intelligent. I want my presidents truly believing that their shit smells sweeter than most. That's why I always liked Mbeki. He always gave that aura of not really wanting to be bothered with the whining and carrying on of the toiling masses. That's the type of president who makes it possible for me to snuggle in bed in the foetal position with a thumb in my mouth and sleep peacefully. I don't want a president who's just like me. The idea of a president who is more or less as knowledgeable as I am scares the living crap out of me. I want to know that while I sleep, my president has got this whole governance thing covered. I want him in a nightgown, pipe in mouth, searching for answers on the World Wide Web.

And so back to reality. What do we have? Well, we have a bunch of mediocre individuals and loads of below-average plonkers in parliament. The criteria for being part of the almost 300 ANC MPs in parliament is that one must have struggle credentials. That's correct; that seems to be the most popular qualification to be a member of the parliamentary portfolio committee on Trade and Industry. Having prepared Molotov cocktails to launch on hostel dwellers on Katlehong's infamous Khumalo Street or rendered the Fort Hare campus ungovernable so as to bring Oupa Gqozo's regime to its knees seems to get one a free pass to control multimillion-rand budgets.

If it sounds like I'm bitter about not qualifying for a position in parliament, it's probably because I am. Unfortunately I did not have the foresight to be part of the struggle when I had the opportunity. I did, however, make a bit of an effort to do things that could be vaguely termed "activism". But truth be told, I was a lousy comrade. That's because the true reason I used to attend those pseudo-political events was to gain access to complimentary entertainment and other freebies associated with being a member of clubs and societies. One of the worst-kept secrets around campus was that the groupies who hung around SRC offices always put out. Other perks included guzzling SRC-funded brandy-and-coke while zigzagging the country in SRC-funded vehicles and intermittently crashing said vehicles. I know a guy who left my Durban campus in an SRC kombi apparently headed for a conference in the Western Cape. But he opted to take a scenic route that culminated in his ride expiring a few kilometres from his village of origin in Giyani in the Limpopo province. Limpopo always features quite strongly in *The Daily Sun* headlines. Perhaps he was abducted by a gang of sex-crazed tokoloshes who took turns sodomising him and guzzling his SRC-funded stash of alcohol, which ultimately led to the accident.

And so, what form did this "political activism" on campus take that has secured the correct struggle credentials for so many of today's low-IQ genius MPs? It was mostly a whole lot of nothingness from a bunch of pathological liars who used to start meetings with cryptic sentences uttered in hushed tones. "Comrades, at this critical juncture in our revolution, we have got word from the leadership in Lusaka." It took me years to realise that "word from Lusaka" meant that some insomniac comrade had been fiddling with his portable radio searching for Radio Bophuthatswana on AM when he inadvertently stumbled upon a station that may or may not have been a broadcast of the ANC's Radio Freedom through the snap-crackle-pop. It was also common for a comrade to disappear for a semester and return to campus with "word from Lusaka" when he had, in fact, gone AWOL upon realising that he had not satisfied exam entrance requirements, spending six months at home in Madadeni, Newcastle, guzzling sorghum beer with shebeen harlots.

These are some of the comrades making all the decisions today. I met some of them at the 52nd ANC National Conference in Polokwane back in December 2007. The *Mail & Guardian* online team were in an experimental mood and wanted to see what would happen if they sent someone without any journalistic integrity, common decency or credibility to cover the event. The five-day period I spent at the ANC Polokwane conference is the closest I think I will ever come to attending a *Star Trek* convention in Las Vegas. For starters, some brilliant mind decided to hold the conference in what I was reliably told was the largest marquee ever assembled in the history of humankind on a University of Limpopo sports field. Each time I walked in there was a *Starship Enterprise* feel about it.

On one end was a podium with mostly overweight, ashen-faced individuals in an assortment of green, black and gold garb and paraphernalia. The Council of the Starship Enterprise. On the floor of the marquee were about 4,000 individuals engaged in either singing, toyi-toying or hurling insults at each other. That's because, as the media contingent soon found out, the ANC branch members were in the grips of the most advanced case of gangsta mentality ever recorded in the 95-year history of the organisation. And there were two sides: the Zuma camp and the Mbeki camp. In keeping with the *Star Trek* theme, let's call them the Borg and the Klingons. It was riveting stuff. Especially the very first session where the Borg spent the morning shouting at "Terrified" Lekota to sit his ass down. From what I could gather, both gangs wanted their preferred leaders to emerge as the new captain of the *Starship Enterprise*.

But that was the end of the entertainment for the rest of the week. Next up was the absolute lowlight of the whole big, damp squib. Something called "The president speaks" took place in the afternoon. For all my respect for former president Thabo Mbeki and his "intellectual traditions", I have always thought of him as a bit of a bore. What nobody had ever told me is the fact that Mbeki has the personality of a dehydrated mopane worm carcass. I have known flowerpots with more charisma. He proceeded to read from a 42-page speech so mind-numbingly tedious that two hours into the thing I would have gladly surrendered to an alien spaceship knowing that I would spend a week being given a sulphuric-acid enema. Karima Brown of *Business Day*, one of the sharpest political analysts in the country, was seated on the floor just to my right. I think she would probably have gladly pulled the pin herself if I had shoved a grenade inside her mouth to put her out of her misery. She spent the entire time stabbing herself in the leg with a sharp pencil to keep awake.

I remember scribbling on my notepad, "What the effing eff is going on in this man's mind?" Here is someone fighting for his political survival, a legacy that he has spent all his life building, and he's trying to put everybody to sleep? Or maybe the plan was to hypnotise everybody? For a man with Mbeki's reported appreciation for history, I had imagined that I would be listening to a riveting Churchillian "We shall fight them on the beaches" type speech. Members of his Klingon tribe groaned audibly and the Borg just sat there impassively, completely oblivious to the pockets of heavily statistically slanted hot air emanating from Mbeki's mouth. They sat there patiently just waiting for the moment they would cast their votes.

Honk If You Feel Your Taxes Aren't Working For You

"Resistance is futile, you will be assimilated," they seemed to radiate from every pore.

And so RIP Thabo Mbeki's political career. I think that the Council of the Starship Enterprise could have saved everybody a lot of valuable festive-season time and a lot of money if delegates had arrived in the morning, cast their votes and went home. That's all anybody was interested in. And that, quite frankly, is about it insofar as democracy is concerned: casting votes.

Many people agree with me. But they're too obsessed with staying politically correct to vocalise their disgruntlement with the outcomes of democratic processes because democracy is as sacrosanct as Jesus' divinity. It's been a year and some months since the last national ANC conference and people are still seriously upset with the results. Here's a fact folks: the outcomes of that conference were the epitome of what "democracy at work" means. Perhaps the ANC has never experienced, and may never experience, a more democratic conference – allowing the will of the majority to be heard. My man Thabo Mbeki was previously elected unopposed, both in 1997 and 2002. Jacob Zuma was elected by the people in a fair contest. Yes, those people were ANC delegates – and unless you live in cuckoo land, ANC delegates represent what 70 per cent of South Africans want. No other grouping comes close to mirroring the "will of the people". It's called democracy. The moment you question that decision, you're starting to ask, "But are they even qualified to make that decision?"

Either you accept their decision or you join me in giving the middle finger to "the people". It's your move.

If it sounds like I am picking on the ANC, it's probably because I am. I feel that I am entitled to it for all the times I have put my cross next to their logo. So what about the rest of the street gangs? I don't even know where to start with that nondescript collection of streetwalkers and pimps who go by the broad term "opposition parties". Who are these people and why are they in the Houses of Parliament? Does anybody know? Do they themselves have a clue? Or is their job to sit there, wait for the ANC to propose something predictably ludicrous like renaming Durban's Point Road to Mahatma Ghandi Street and then oppose it? For the record, I wish that whichever anti-Indian racist proposed the naming of that urine-stained stretch of debauchery after one of the world's foremost champions for human rights goes straight to hell. It is criminal that R5 hookers are peddling their wrinkled, saggy wares on the Mahatma.

Speaking of prostitution, back to the opposition parties whose ideologically flexible members have been known to whore themselves to the highest bidder come floor-crossing time. (The fact that it took them six years to realise the flaw in that process rather supports my theory of the calibre of individuals who constitute parliament.) I think that the term "opposition parties" is part of the problem here. What is now happening is that any unimaginative, unemployed individual wants to be in parliament so he can go oppose the ANC. That's all our opposition parties ever do. In fact, in the past I have argued that we do not need political analysts who are experts on ANC internal matters. Parliament is filled with a bunch of overrated ANC analysts masquerading as politicians. If you don't believe me, go to Google and type "Helen Zille + ANC" and be dazzled by the fact that you have 7,876,456 links popping up. Ditto Patricia de Lille or Bantu Holomisa or any of the others. I do not believe that any of these people have ever uttered three sentences in a row without mentioning the ANC. I wonder if any of them actually have any of their own independently constructed policies. If they put together a survey, asked our 22 million or so voters to tell me in one sentence what the DA stands for that the ID doesn't, I bet there'd be a lot of blank scripts coming back. The one thing they have in common is telling the electorate that it is the inherent ANCness of the ANC that makes them fuck up. I'm not convinced. I think it is the politician in them. And unfortunately, being a human being is not a prerequisite for being a politician.

Unfortunately for us, the citizens of this country, we are stuck with this democratic monster. It is US foreign policy to ensure that as much of the world as possible remains democratic despite the spectacular failure of this system in so many different lands. I mean, when they vote in George

Honk If You Feel Your Taxes Aren't Working For You

W Bush not once, but twice, well, surely that's saying something right there?

So this democracy experiment will continue unabated. The double-chinned guys and gals will assemble in parliament passing motions of no confidence on the parliamentary committee responsible for the operationalisation of the implementation strategy as contained in the White paper of 2004, which integrated all the policy documents that had been adopted to harmonise the efforts to strengthen governmental interventions towards the complete alleviation of poverty among the poorest of the poor in line with the principles enshrined in clause 341 of paragraph 31 (version 37) of our Constitution of 1996. Or something along those lines. A great deal of verbal flatulence will rise up to the heavens amidst lots of acrimonious name-calling. It will all make for riveting viewing in the mould of David Attenborough on his tummy regaling us about the mating habits of the praying mantis.

And that's my way of saying that this whole system is not working for me. Every year the government takes about 25 per cent of my income. Of the rest of the 75 per cent, they take a further 14 per cent each time I make a purchase. Then they take more each time I try to drive anywhere. Add it all up and I am left with 23 cents on the rand. It is a legalised form of mugging. By the time they're done I feel like a turtle on its back struggling to get up with my boxers around my ankles. A democratic government is, by design, not capable of delivering anything tangible for reasons so eloquently elucidated on in this academic paper you're reading. I feel that people who take three-quarters of my money every year should at least be a little entertaining. Is it too much to ask that these muggers stop pretending that they are there for anybody else but themselves? What the hell am I paying 77 per cent for?

When the parliamentary finance portfolio committee chairman, Nhlanhla Nene, fell off his chair – bless you, YouTube – I personally felt it was a good start. I think I watched that clip about 250 times within a few hours of receiving it. I was in a good mood the entire day. I felt like my taxes were working for me. I was entertained. And then I started thinking why we, the people, cannot insist that the whole lot of them sit on precariously perched high chairs with hot-air detectors at least once a week. And when a critical mass of hot air has been emitted, the chair breaks. I do believe that this is the gist of Boyle's Law: the more a body releases hot air, the higher its specific gravity and the higher the likelihood of chairs buckling. I'd feel like my PAYE and VAT were working for me, then.

Bugger it, I'd be willing to pay an extra tax – call it the Public Entertainment Tax (PET) – just to watch Makhenkesi Stofile run around the Loftus pitch chasing around a springbok in that body suit Kgotso Mokoena was wearing during his Olympic silver medal-winning performance. Stofile is notorious for his obsession with those thingamagoats called springboks, so how about he runs around like one? A Sports Minister who engages in physical exertions on national TV. Imagine that.

Wouldn't you feel that the PET tax was worth it if the public were allowed to make a human chain outside parliament with a bucket of rotten eggs per citizen, pelting our MPs as they arrived for the State of the Nation address? Imagine the well-heeled fat cats in their shiny suits being forced to walk through a quicksand pit to access the inside of the Union Buildings. Wouldn't that make you feel all warm inside? I'd certainly feel much better about the fact that I pay all that money and yet the pothole in front of my gate has not been fixed in two years. But of course, in a democracy, we would never have any of that.

I don't reckon I'm getting my money's worth here. Am I all alone? Do you feel your taxes are working for you?

Is It Coz I'm Black?

Music: The True Opium Of The Masses

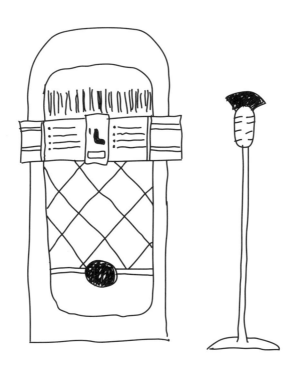

It seems that I have always been surrounded by music. My father, EB Ngcobo, is possibly the most musical human being I have ever encountered. Besides being a school principal, he was also a choir conductor and choral music composer of note. He even had an album with some original material cut at the SABC when he conducted the choir of the Ukusa High School of Mpumalanga Township in Hammarsdale. When my elder brother Mazwi was born, my father wrote a song about it titled "Umntwana", the mention of which, to this very day, causes my brother to grin from ear to ear. (No-one has ever written a song about me yet, but I'm working on it.)

Every Saturday morning we woke up to the sounds of Miriam Makeba's "Suliram" and "Olilili", Ella Fitzgerald's "Brighten The Corner Where You Are", Babsy Mlangeni's "Mina Ngiyaphila" and Elvis Presley's "Are You Lonesome Tonight?" wafting through the house, courtesy of my mother's extensive LP and '45 collection. She loved those old tunes, my mom.

The more cynical reader may well have concluded by now that the obvious point of all of this harmonious nostalgia is to brag about my old man's accomplishments and my mother's fine musical taste so as to create a distinctive aura of great musical heritage around myself. Well spotted. Indeed, when it comes to music, my parents certainly taught me well. But nobody ever told me that music is a supremely dangerous mind-altering entity significantly more potent than most banned substances. I am not kidding.

The first time I was introduced to music's potential as a powerful narcotic was during the politically turbulent year of 1986. At the time, my tiny conservative Catholic high school in Vryheid in northern Natal did not have a history of political activism, despite producing an impressive number of high-profile activists and (later) being pretty well represented in cabinet and public institutions. But a politicised young monk, at the time a seminarian at Pietermaritzburg's St Joseph's Theological School in Cedara, took it upon himself to introduce some of us to struggle politics.

What a lot of people do not quite appreciate about struggle politics is the role played by song in whipping activists into the appropriate mood.

It takes more than just strong political convictions to walk around with a hand grenade in your pocket. After spending about two hours sloganeering and singing liberation songs, we toyi-toyi'd around campus during which time I found myself with uncontrollable urges to set buildings – and other general stuff – on fire. As luck would have it I did not have access to any oil-based fuel, a crucial ingredient in manufacturing Molotov cocktails. To this day, I have no idea why I wanted to burn things so badly. But I do have a vivid recollection of fantasising about sticking a red-hot stainless-steel wire up PW Botha's urethra. That is the power of music.

Walking around the Polokwane campus of the University of Limpopo during the 52nd ANC conference in December 2007, I was reminded of that moment from 21 years earlier. Singing was very much the order of the day, with the opposing factions hellbent on outperforming the other side. After a few days I realised that I was walking around humming "Umshini Wami" under my breath. And liking it. That's a catchy-ass tune right there. I bet if I was a member of the ANC Youth League who'd listened to the song a few thousand times, I'd probably be quite keen on killing for JZ myself. A young lady journalist shook her head sadly and made sarcastic comments about the folly of it all. Surely the elections for the top positions would not be decided on the basis of song, she observed sarcastically. I felt like hitting her on the back of her head with a rolled-up copy of *Umrabulo*, the ANC magazine, to knock some sense into her. Was she not aware that our ancestors from thousands of years ago had been sophisticated enough to understand the power of song in striking the fear of God into the hearts of our enemies? Or that song is the order of the day in Catholic parishes across the globe? That's because Catholic Church leaders are acutely aware of the cause-and-effect connection between song and an open heart to the Word. And the propensity to deposit R50 notes in the collection plate, of course. Ditto most other religious formations.

It is for these reasons that I like to point out to people that the phrase "trance music" is a redundancy – because all music induces a trancelike state to a certain degree. Every young man who has ever gone out on a date is acutely aware of the mood-altering power of music. Marvin Gaye and Teddy Pendergrass played a pivotal role in getting many of my dates to shed their knickers when I was a horny young man. As a result, five bars of any Nat King Cole song elicit strong feelings of love inside of me to this very day. Equally, I get satanic urges to guzzle cobra blood and trash hotel rooms when I listen to a couple of bars of any Metallica song.

Abraham Maslow (1908-1970) is an American dude of Russian-Jewish descent who hypothesised that human beings are unlikely to get the urge to have a porn festival on their home-theatre systems until they've had pork chops and taken a whizz first. This he wrote in his 1943 paper, "A Theory of Human Motivation". This theory is popularly known as Maslow's Hierarchy of Needs. The geek clearly never went on too many dates. Where does a man get the time to worry about this sort of nonsense? But he had a point. It would seem that there is indeed a correlation between a full tummy and the acute uncontrollable urge for beauty, symmetry and soothing sounds. I think he called these urges aesthetic needs. Music is one of these.

Because scientists love to feel important and reinforce their bogus know-it-all statuses, various attempts have been made to come up with an explanation for the feelings of euphoria brought about by a remarkable work of art. Why does looking at that sculpture make you ever so content? Why do you feel joy while listening to Beethoven? Or Beyoncé? Apparently it has something to do with the production of some protein-based opioid chemicals, which are second cousins of the opium family and commonly known as endorphins. Whatever the real BS-less reason, I think we've all had this rush of blood to the head – or the groin as the case may be – when exposed to our favourite music.

Some people find this titillation in paintings. I must confess that I've never quite appreciated this form of creativity. It may have something to do with a personality disorder that precludes me from receiving that endorphin rush upon gazing at a painting of a woman with eight buttocks as popularised by Pablo Picasso. I'm not sure, to be honest. Either way, paintings are out. And movies, too. Once upon a time I used to enjoy going to the cinema. But that was before movie theatres were invaded en masse by armies of Eminem wannabees in baggy jeans around their ankles who smell of a mixture of goats-in-heat and Axe. Long story involving me almost roundhouse-kicking one of the Axe Brigade in the groin and punching him in the solar plexus inside a Durban mall.

So, as it turns out, most of my opioid rushes seem to emanate from good music. It is appropriate, therefore, that every major milestone in my life has a song associated with it. For one, my passage into manhood brings a distinctive tune to mind. You might be forgiven for thinking that I'm referring to a war chant that my fellow initiates and I belted out in the Transkei mountains while covered in skins and smeared in cow dung. But no – wrong Nguni grouping. My passage to manhood occurred under far less propitious circumstances. I was in the study at my Catholic boarding school in the middle of nowhere a few months after my 13th birthday. I was supposed to be busy with my Afrikaans homework but I was in fact deeply engrossed in the vivid description of a liaison between a hero and a female known as Lorelei as artistically depicted by that great American novelist Louis L'amour – with my other hand in my pants. That's when I inadvertently discovered that I had joined the reproductive section of the population – rather explosively. Somewhere in the background the recently released Temptations album *Truly For You* was blaring.

For the next few months this excellent music was to serve as the background for many other important, albeit less explosive, milestones. This was the first Temptations album after the departure of leading vocalist Dennis Edwards (of "Papa Was A Rolling Stone" fame). The music was as rhythmic, flowing and smooth as ever, with Ron Tyson's voice leading the graceful harmonies with hits such as "Treat Like A Lady", "How Can You Say" and my personal, personal favourite, "I'll Keep My Light In My Window". The endorphins flowed inside my brain like the tears from Pirates fans after Chiefs have snatched the Premiership from them.

And then, as is in the nature of these things, The Temptations were forgotten as we all moved on to superior music in the form of the Michael Jacksons and, ultimately, the Milli Vanillis of this world. Those were the bad ol' days. As is always the case with really good songs, "I'll Keep My

Light In My Window" had never really been uprooted from my mind – it was merely buried under the rubble. And that fine song re-emerged and started playing over and over in my head around the mid-'90s. We were already deep into the digital era by that time so I set out on a mission to get my hands on the CD.

I wonder if I'm the only one who's had this happen to me. You walk into the music shop. You know what music you want. You know the artist. Hell, you can hear the bloody song playing inside your mind. But for the life of you, you have no idea what the title of the song is. But by sunny Jesus and Holy Mary mother of God, you are absolutely determined to get through to the purple-headed assistant with a nose-ring behind the Musica counter that you need this particular piece of music. So you stand there in your suit and tie inside the music shop with other patrons milling about, and you give Purplehead over there an impromptu *Idols* performance:

Some call me foolish
To lend a helping hand
So I'll keep my light in my window
Oh oh oh!
I feel so good when I help my fellow man
So I'll keep my light in my window
Oh oh oh!

"You know that song, right?"

Of course, by this time, your singing voice – which is a cross between a scream from a bullfrog falling through the branches of a thorn tree and an ejaculating alley cat – has attracted half a dozen curious onlookers. Some of them are ready to jump up and perform the Heimlich manoeuvre on you because they think you're choking on a chicken wing. To rub salt into the wound, Purplehead starts messing around with you.

"Yes, sir, I think we have that song. Just sing it to me one more time. Hey guys, a customer needs help – come listen to this!"

That's right, he's calling his colleagues from the back of the store so they can have a really good chuckle at your expense. Because you're not actually an idiot, you can see what's happening – and yet you go ahead, undeterred. You need this song because you haven't had a really good endorphin fix in a while. So you're gonna get that light in that freaking window, goddamnit, if it's the last thing you do…

By around the year 2000, I was ready to give up on the damn song. I had spent hundreds of man-hours scouring the pits of the World Wide Web in search of the album. I had, by now, established that it had never been digitally mastered, which meant that the few copies I was encountering on the internet from far away places in Eastern Europe, for $200 a shot, were vinyls. I'm ashamed to say that by 2002 I was ready to give my credit card details to an individual called Bozorgmehr from Andizhan in Uzbekistan. But by this time I didn't care; I was like a crackhead desperate for just one drag. If someone had walked up to me on the corner of Rissik and Jeppe in downtown Jozi and told me they had a cassette tape recording of "I'll Keep My Light In My Window", I would have gladly handed over my entire wallet and slaughtered a medium-sized horned mammal in homage to the ancestors afterwards.

The first breakthrough in the quest to relieve my pain occurred in the spring of 2002. Or so I thought. It was a Sunday morning and my wife – then my girlfriend – and I were in the car en route to wherever the hell women drag hungover men on Sunday mornings as punishment. My sweetheart was fiddling with the radio stations when she inadvertently passed over the 96.4 FM frequency. That's Metro FM to the culturally challenged. And then she moved on… I immediately emitted a bloodcurdling scream reminiscent of Tarzan passing a kidney stone. Something along the lines of, "AAAAIIIIAAAIIIAAA, stupid woman! Back to Metro FM goddamnit!"

She got such a fright that she stepped on the accelerator and went through a red robot before coming to a screeching halt on the other side. I didn't care. This was a moment I was willing to die for. My eyes were closed, fingers snapping and I was singing along over the 500kW

Music: The True Opium Of The masses **101**

speakers:

To make this world a better place
For me and you-hoo-hoo-hoo-hoo-hoo-hoooo...

To those who are uninitiated to the world of black radio, Wilson B Nkosi is one of Metro FM's stalwarts, the longest-serving presenter on that urban radio station, having been there since its humble beginnings, circa 1986. He hosts the Sunday 9am to 12pm slot cryptically titled "Sounds And Stuff Like That". It's a soul-classics show. Nkosi makes up for his mundane musings about what goes on in his head and his punchline-less jokes that only he finds funny with a great appreciation for classic soul music. And on this Sunday morning I was ready to forgive him for the sins he had been committing against the entire art of poetry for years. I sat there in the car listening to the harp-like guitar rhythms of The Temptations and the haunting harmony with my face raised to the sky like a madman while my future wife sat there reconsidering her options.

That very Sunday afternoon I made my first attempt at getting hold of Wilson B Nkosi for the purpose of having him point me in the direction of the source of his copy. I emailed. Then I called. Then I emailed again. Then I promised fellatio. Nothing. Nada. I even went to a shady Daveyton Township tavern where he was playing one Sunday afternoon to try to persuade him to reveal his secret. I think he was starting to consider putting a restraining order on my stalker ass so I executed a strategic retreat to go lick my wounds. I hadn't even managed a 30-second conversation with the man.

Soon, the sadistic bastard was playing the song every fourth or fifth Sunday – with no discernible pattern. I think he did it just to fuck with me. Each Sunday I was subjecting myself to three hours of Wilson reading such bad poetry on air it made Mzwakhe Mbuli seem like a bona fide Mafika Pascal Gwala. All so I could possibly catch the four minutes or so of my song.

The second false breakthrough occurred recently, in 2006. By this time, my wife and I had been living in Pinetown, west of Durban, for about two years. Our immediate neighbour in our cluster-home complex was a hefty woman whose motto in life seemed to be "Neighbours are the spawn of the devil" which, conveniently for us, was a sentiment we shared. On the Sunday in question I was sitting outside on the patio minding my own business when I heard the first bars of "How Can You Say", from *Truly For You*, the same Temptations album that features my desired "I'll Keep My Light In My Window". I took a large gulp, choked on my beer and sat up like a mutt hearing the sweet sounds of a bitch in heat howling down the street. There was the unmistakable crackle of a needle on vinyl. Ohmygod! Could it be? "How Can You Say" finished, and then… *my song*! My wife had to physically restrain me from jumping over the tiny fence separating our houses and giving that big, angry woman a bear hug. At that moment I was willing to bribe her for that song using every resource at my disposal. Money, parking space, playing sperm donor for her future little tubs of lard – anything.

Sanity prevailed and I restrained myself. But of course now I saw my neighbour in a different light. Nobody who owns that album could be all that bad. My soul's appetite had been whetted and I had to gain access to the woman next door. (No, not *that* type of access.) So I started engaging in a dangerous game. Now each time we happened to come out of our houses at the same time, I'd smile and wave. Next thing I knew I had made some inroads. Now we were chitchatting a little bit if we met at the gate on garbage-collection day. Real cosy but just short of an emotional affair. With my bowling pins all set up, I was ready to knock them down.

One windy Tuesday afternoon, armed with a yearning for my artistic soul to be fed, I approached her door. I needed that endorphin rush badly. I knocked nervously, told her my sob story and wondered out loud if she would be willing to break our intellectual-property laws by lending me her LP record to have it digitally recorded. And, of course, I'd make a CD copy for her if it so pleased her. I begged. I cajoled.

"No," she declared. She had a better idea. "Why don't you come back another day with some cassette tapes and we can have ourselves a jolly time recording these tunes." Er, okay, I responded weakly, imagining my wife's concerned look when I told her I'd be going next door to have a soul-classics session with the heavy-bosomed woman we prefer to ignore. And so that dream disappeared like scones from a plate at a parent-teacher meeting.

It would be another year before my search for "I'll Keep My Light In My Window" came to a glorious end. A friend of mine I like to call Shorty sent me a link to a website from which I could legitimately download the entire album for about $2.50. Easy as that. Oh joy! Now I had an MP3 with one of my favourite songs of all time and I could merrily drive my wife, kids, the neighbours' dogs, friends and enemies alike to distraction. Ah! Sheer bliss.

I have tried to share this song with everyone I have met, with varying success. Some of my friends love it. Quite a few can't stand it. I even had someone point out to me that I am just a slave to junk American music, and why couldn't I be proudly South African? Black people like to say things like that, especially in politically correct company. Later, you'll likely discover that the individual giving you all that crap has the greatest collection of American jazz CDs this side of the equator. Not that there's anything wrong with the noble notion of supporting South African music. And we have great musicians here. I know some of them personally. It's just that they, too, have extensive American music collections. It seems that most people I know have an affinity for music from that part of the world.

Of course, human beings being humans, even music is not immune to idiocy. While I've just insisted that everybody listens to crap American music, black people listen to black American crap, while white people listen to white American crap. (Yes, yes, obviously there are exceptions. But let's just ignore these for the time being and stick to my new rule. This is called generalising.) What most white people don't know is that most of us darkies think music is our exclusive domain. It's quite common to hear one of us throw this insult at another darkie: "You sing like a freaking whitey." And honest whiteys acknowledge it, too. That's why the white band Gecko Moon could not find a better lead singer than Ringo Madlingozi. Ditto Zolani Mahola of Freshlyground. Show me a whitey who can hold a candle to Aretha Franklin, Roberta Flack, Stevie Wonder or Donny Hathaway in the vocal stakes and I'll show you a vegetarian hyena.

Not that all whiteys can't sing, of course. Some white singers seriously piss me off because they're more than just a little good. I will even sheepishly admit that part of my music collection includes Frank Sinatra, Barbra Streisand, The Carpenters, Sting, U2, George Michael, Crowded House and that new irritating little soulful twerp called Robin Thicke. White people who can sing... Must they have everything? You don't see some black dude challenging Ryk Neethling in the pool, do you? Brothers don't float too good and whiteys can't hold a tune. We stick to our side of the bargain; why can't you stick to yours? What's next? Some dude with surfer hair taking out Usain Bolt in the 100m dash?

Before I go off the deep end as I normally do, let me say this: I love music. I love my ballads soulful, soppy-wet and as depressing as hell, and I wish someone out there with some vision would offer me a DJ contract in a fine music station. Preferably the graveyard shift. I'd sit in that studio at 3am opening up the endorphin taps inside every listener's brain, and I'd love every second of it. Is anyone out there listening?

Is It Coz I'm Black?

No Sex, Please! We're Calvinists

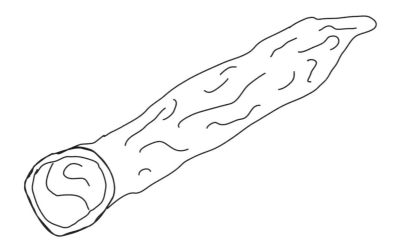

s Kenny gazed deeply into Lerato's large brown eyes, he felt a stirring in his loins of a magnitude he had never experienced before. The intensity of his stare shocked Lerato to her core and she found her whole body shivering with anticipation and longing for his touch. Her heart throbbed. Her breasts heaved. As they entered the filling-station convenience shop, their arms brushed momentarily, sending jolts of electricity through both their bodies.

The store was well stocked; the decision would not be an easy one. "A plethora of safety," thought Kenny. He reached for a packet of regular condoms but stopped short, noting the look of disappointment on Lerato's face. She gestured towards the extra-sensitive Featherlites, enquiring of him with her sensuous eyes. Kenny was touched by her unselfishness. "She wants to maximise my pleasure," he thought. "How thoughtful." So he returned the favour, playfully tossing Lerato a pack of luminous rib-studded condoms. Immediately he knew they had found a winner. She came closer and planted a light kiss of gratitude on his lips while clutching the brightly coloured box between her delicate fingers...

About 15 years ago I hypothesised that condom use would be so rife in the future that it would become infused into everyday life and into popular culture. I used to imagine that love scenes in romance novels would read like the passage above. Kind of. But it would seem that I got it very wrong because the use of condoms today still seems to be a taboo topic of discussion.

As you might imagine, I have particularly strong opinions about sex in general. They go something like this. Sex is a great thing. I'm all for sex in almost all its forms. No, that does not include getting jiggy with Brutus, the family Doberman. (Though, that is, of course, just a subjective, personal preference. You might come from a perspective that says it's cool to make Brutus climb the walls and ululate in ecstasy while you chant, "Fuck the SPCA!" Each to his own.) But I love sex. Period. If I had my way, sex would fill a large chunk of my day; not just those few minutes late at night when I'm ready to collapse from exhaustion. Alas, sex is an endeavour that one should preferably engage in with a partner, and partners are not always up for it. That's not to say that sex by oneself can't be thoroughly enjoyable, too. To quote a boyhood buddy: "The beauty of sex by myself lies in the flexibility it affords me. I can have sex with a virgin if I want to, but when I'm in a Friday-night kind of mood I can get it on with a filthy slapper merely by loosening my grip." It is difficult to argue with such watertight logic.

I really struggle to understand why talking openly about sex is such a no-no in normal society. Of course, I am well aware that I can never be accused of being called normal. I have been known to regale friends with detailed accounts of my forays into the bathroom to execute a number two. But sex is hardly the same as the ejection of excrement. Sex is a beautiful, beautiful thing – despite what John Calvin thought.

For the uninitiated in the constipated thoughts of John Calvin, he was the anally retentive bearded fellow who right royally screwed up many societies across the world with his 16th-century theological opinions. He convinced his many followers that Jesus wants us all to be miserable and to resist the temptation to partake in any activities that might bring us pleasure. Such as sex. If I were president of the world for a day I'd have his body exhumed, subjected to a firing squad and hanged upside down by his nads on Mary Fitzgerald Square. Him and a succession of those purple-robed pious men with tiny hats from the Vatican.

While feeling rather strongly about this, I am also acutely aware that, as great as sex is, the 21st-century version is also fraught with mortal danger at every hot-and-sweaty turn. Especially in these parts. Still, when I first heard that our president-in-waiting Jacob Zuma had admitted to having sex with an HIV-positive woman without using a condom, my reaction was quite off-centre. At the time, I merely shrugged and said, "Yeah, so what." My primary concern was not AIDS-related; it was whether or not the sex was consensual – because anybody who forces himself on someone else rightly deserves to lose his puny poor excuse for a member. Preferably by means of a blunt butter knife. And I'm deadly serious about that – as serious as the wave of nausea that often hits me at 3am after an

No Sex, Please! We're Calvinists **109**

evening in the company of eight Castle draughts.

That said, I still struggle to understand why Zuma's intellect has been doubted by so many because of his "decision" to go ahead and plunge into the crevices of a woman carrying a deadly virus. The quote marks on "decision" are because I question the decision-making skills of human brain cells directly after a mass exodus of blood to the genitals. I'd hazard the suggestion that not much thinking happens at that point. As a result, JZ's intellect had nothing to do with it, I'd say. And I'll venture, too, that nature or our Maker – depending on your religious beliefs or non-beliefs – exhibited the wisdom of Solomon in designing us this way. Because I believe that our instincts to get naked and conjoin our Jacks and Jills are hard-wired into that part of the brain that does not house logic and rationality. And I think we're built like that for a very good reason. The human species surely would not have thrived if we had the ability to reason during the state of sexual arousal. There most certainly wouldn't be six billion of us and counting today.

Imagine if, for example, Hitler's dad-to-be had possessed the ability to look at Hitler's mom-to-be as she was getting naked and think to himself, "I really shouldn't engage in sexual intercourse with this woman. She's got a serious case of crazy eye and she skinned our cat alive last week. She probably shouldn't be allowed to procreate." Little Adolf would never have been born. But his dad just didn't have control over his urges. Even if he did have his doubts, he went ahead anyway, quite possibly yelling, "I'm your daddy and I command you to do that crazy-eye thing of yours that drives me berserk!" as little Adolf was conceived. Never mind that Hitler went on to put a good dent in that human population I was talking about. The point I'm making is that when it's time to get it on, men and women tend to overlook the rationalising side of things.

You may have read to here and figured I'm talking gibberish because you think you have the ability to reason under a state of sexual arousal. Let's interrogate this for a second. Can we all agree that the following scenario is very common and that it involves what most people consider to be rational behaviour? Boy meets girl inside club [insert meat market of choice here]. Girl locks eyes with boy and decides that she has no problems shedding her panties for him, and vice versa (assuming he's wearing panties). Boy and girl drive to boy's place. Seeing as boy and girl do not know each other from a can of paint, one of them produces a packet of condoms, and they spend the rest of the early morning locked in a passionate embrace and having great sex. Or lousy sex, as the case may be.

Here is where things get a little fuzzy for me. Let's assume you're the boy in the above scenario. You just met this girl two hours ago. You have no idea where she's been and who she's been there with. Because of your ignorance on the details of her life, the most prudent thing to do is to make the assumption that she's carrying a dangerous, deadly virus in her bodily fluids. So far, so good – you cannot fault the logic. But things get a little weird from this point on. Based on your completely rational assumption that ignorance on her HIV status is exactly the same as her being infected, you then make an ostensibly logical decision. Faced with the choice between going home alone and sleeping with her, you go ahead and sleep with her using a 50-micron-thick prophylactic barrier between your skin and her presumably potentially deadly fluids. Scientific studies have shown that the use of the ultra-thin layer of latex has a 97 per cent efficacy in preventing the transfer of her fluids into yours, after all. And you're willing to gamble on the 3 per cent probability that the 50-micron barrier will protect you. Okay, I guess that makes 97 per cent sense.

Where it gets really interesting for me is when we start drilling down into your presumably rational stance. What if I ask you whether you would go ahead and sleep with a woman if I told you as a matter of fact that she was HIV positive? If you say no, as I suspect most people would, can you reconcile that "decision" with the "decision" to go ahead based on nothing but your ignorance of the woman's status? Can we agree that using a condom when you don't know is tantamount to an admission that your partner is as good as infected as far as you are concerned? Because if I told you with absolute certainty that the woman was not infected and was on the pill, the likelihood that you would use a condom is greatly diminished, isn't it? Isn't that what happens when people get married; that is, they take tests and then toss the condoms aside?

Before you have me hauled off to Mary Fitzgerald Square to be subjected to the John Calvin treatment, allow me to clarify what I'm saying. I'm not suggesting that people follow the example of our high-calibre political leadership and ride bareback on the plains of HIV, yelling "Yee-haa!". That would just be irresponsible. All I'm doing is pointing out the fact that just as we ride on the high horse of righteous indignation at the intellectual bankruptcy of Mr Umshiniwami, we are blinded to our very own stunted thinking. But most of all, dare I suggest that most of us are quite disingenuous about our practice of safe sex while we stand in condemnation of those whose private lives have been laid bare in the public domain?

At a recent gathering of the nondescript, uncouth and uncivilised riffraff I call my friends, I decided to play devil's advocate. "Men Of Thirst!" I cried out (for this is what the savages call themselves: Men Of Thirst or MOT). "Why do we do this to each other?" I asked. "Why do we go around spreading stories about our lives that we know are obvious fabrications?" I then went on to point out how I had been spending quite a bit of time at one of our large hospitals in Ekurhuleni, where one of the members of the MOT is adding value as a healthcare professional. During one of these visits I had taken the time to pay a visit to the antenatal clinic – amusingly known as the ANC – and what I witnessed caused me some serious internal dissonance.

The ANC was packed to the hilt with young women, all carrying buns at varying states of progression. The waiting area sported a long, winding queue of 27 April 1994 proportions. Big ones. Little ones. High-sitting ones. Low-lying ones. And I found myself asking no-one in particular, "Who is fathering all these kids?" To hear the story being told by men all over the place, everybody is practising safe sex. Every time I hear one of these young single guns telling heroic tales of their conquests, there is always a deliberate reference to "…and then I slipped on the rubber…" And yet somehow, here I was inside the hospital's ANC bulging at the seams with women who had clearly been blessed with the holy seed.

So I spoke to my friends from the heart. "MOT," I pleaded, "it is time that we stop fooling ourselves. The lies have to stop. I'm sufficiently open-minded to believe in miracles of biblical proportions. I'm willing to believe that some of the women I saw at the ANC were zapped by Immaculate Conception. And I'm even willing to accept the possibility of the existence of a Knock-em-up Fairy who flies from house to house in the middle of the night, ensuring the survival of the species." Then I paused for effect, studying their inebriated faces before continuing. "But I believe that people like yourselves are also responsible for the queue at the ANC. Confess your sins!"

Slowly, the tales of shame emerged, one by one. At first, the stories were of the usual pathological-liar variety about condoms bursting in the middle of the act. With a bit more encouragement, these lies were swept aside with the observation that, however well-endowed the fellows might be, these stories of sub-strength condoms just had to stop. Emboldened by some pretty candid confessions from one of the MOT, others followed suit. This particular Thirsty Man conceded how he had been concerned on one occasion that the desire of the pretty young thing he was with might wane somewhat if he stopped to run off and fetch protection, and so he just went ahead anyway. He revealed how it was only at the point of extreme ecstasy and pig-like grunting that his mind seemed to return from the place where all minds wander to during sexual arousal. And how he had panicked, run to the bathroom and started wiping his nether regions with a wet Savlon-soaked cloth. Yes, a Savlon-soaked cloth. And we're talking about a seriously smart dude here. The rest of the MOT listened with straight faces, stifling giggles when he went on to explain how he had even gone as far as having himself admitted to a hospital with acute panic-induced hyperventilation.

I personally think it was an important moment for us to have. I think that the conspiracy of silence around sex has got to go. There are too many lies doing the rounds. Especially about black men. I remember how, some years ago, I wandered into a 7/11 on Durban's Esplanade to

No Sex, Please! We're Calvinists   113

purchase a packet of condoms. The owner of the shop was an elderly white gentleman who spoke fluent Zulu. As I stood there trying to decide which variety to purchase, he reached for an exotic pack I had never seen before and quipped, *"Ngiyakubona wena nsizwa ukuthi uyinkunzi yohlobo, iBhulamane loqobo. Udinga amakhondomu anje."* [I can see that you're a real stud bull, a regular Brahman. These are the condoms you need.] The racist pig! I'm sorry, but it's just wrong calling another man a stud Brahman bull. Just coz I'm black!

Okay, maybe it's because our self-perpetuated reputation precedes us. A few years ago, then-president Mbeki delivered a scathing, venomous harangue on this whole notion that there was something peculiar about black men's sexuality. On this point, I agree with the little man. I most certainly have never asked for this reputation. But more than anything else, I don't want it. It's just way too much pressure. I'm just another human male who has good days and bad days. Okay, mostly bad days and a few good days.

Another friend of mine, struggling under the yoke of too much expectation, captured it best. He shared with me how he had spent the evening with a woman who expected miracles from him just because she had "heard great things" about Shangaan men. My buddy tells me how, around 3am, his whole body aching from the exertions of trying to please the ungrateful harlot and with sweat pouring from every pore on his body, he had sternly told her that he was sleeping now. His parting shot, so to speak, was, *"Ha! Phela nami ngiwumuntu nginenyama negazi!"* [That's it! I'm just human with flesh and blood!]

I cannot agree more. This stereotype of the insatiable Energiser Bunny black man must be stamped out. And we, black men, need to stand up and be counted in collective condemnation.

As mentioned in an earlier chapter, one of the barbers I use goes by the name Bab' Nzama. I often visit him at the Watville hostel in Benoni to have my skull shaved under those makeshift tents. He is a stout Zulu man and is a jack of all trades, also dabbling in the chemical science of medicine dispensing. For years he's been castigating me for my refusal to use his other services with the words, *"We-Fuze, ugcine nini ukuchatha? Uzokushiya umfazi mawenza kanje."* [When was the last time you got an invigorating enema? At this rate, your wife will leave you.]

For the culturally challenged, *ukuchatha* is the regular delivery of a potent performance enhancer by means of the pleasant method of an enema. No lubrication required. It is quite a common practice in the hills and valleys of KwaZulu-Natal. But I am a Zulu man with a personality disorder that precludes me from injecting fluids up my posterior orifice. Fuck virility, I say. That said, to get Bab' Nzama off my back, I finally relented and purchased some of his mixture in a 750ml green bottle with a J&B logo. It's sitting in my garage right now, next to all those useless Verimark products, though I must confess that when I'm going through a particularly bad spell – when my staying power is whittled away to an embarrassing four minutes and 37 seconds on average – I do give the green bottle a lean and hungry look and think, "If only the magic fluid could be orally dispensed."

I am blessed with three young sons. I want them to grow up in a world different to the one I grew up in. I want them to grow up in a world where they will feel free to be honest about their sex lives. I do not want them burdened with stud-bull tags from shrivelled-up white men. This is the 21st century; the bovine references to human beings need to stop. But most of all, I want them to grow up in a world where they can be honest with their peers and with me about the pressures of engaging in responsible behaviour. And this can only happen if we start creating an atmosphere where they can feel comfortable being truthful about it.

As a good, semi-practising Catholic, I believe in the exorcism of demons and evil. So please join me in the exorcism of the demon of silence about what truly goes on in the dark when our collective drawers lie crumpled at the foot of the bed. Let's all chant together:

Be gone John Calvin and your evil ways!
Be gone little men in purple robes and tiny hats!

Be gone Bab' Nzama and your virility medicines!
Be gone bovine-obsessed old white prunes!

No Sex, Please! We're Calvinists

Is It Coz I'm Black?

Of Phallic Traditional Weapons And Estelle Getty

Never ascribe to bad driving that which is adequately explained by sheer, unadulterated stupidity.

– Ndumiso Ngcobo

So it's January 2007 and I'm cruising along at a gentle 140km/h on that stretch of the N1 between Three Sisters and Colesburg, happily minding my own business. My wife is sitting beside me reading a magazine, and our two-year-old son is sleeping contentedly in the back. Because we're good parents and responsible citizens, the boy is strapped into his baby seat and both of us are safely buckled. You know, just in case something happens to this automotive contraption hurtling towards its destination at (lest we forget) 140km/h. Let it never be said that we don't value our lives. Even at 140km/h.

In my rear-view mirror I notice what appears to be a terrestrial NASA spaceship approaching me at somewhere in the region of 700km/h. It is red in colour, has a lowered suspension and a logo with four rings. Because it has broken through the sound barrier, the registration plates have fallen off. (It has been my observation that this is a phenomenon common to many vehicles travelling at these speeds.) To prevent the NASA orbiter from using us as an emergency braking system, I gently slide onto the shoulder of the road, across the yellow line, and reduce my speed to a 100km/h crawl. As he whizzes past us, I catch a glimpse of the human astro-turd at the wheel. His face is so red it is just asking for Manto to grate it, add a dash of olive oil and Jack Daniel's and cure someone of AIDS. He has a Magnum PI-esque moustache and an impressive bottom lip dangling almost to his chest.

The trouble starts when the BMW in front of us, also travelling along at a sedate 140km/h, does not give way to the earthbound Apollo. Our ever-thoughtful Neil Armstrong flicks his headlights furiously at the Beemer. Nothing. He's not budging. More flicking of lights. Nada. The nose of the Audi is almost touching the BMW's tail at a now-improved speed of about 180km/h, judging by the increasing gap between our car and the Germans. And then the oncoming lane clears up. The Audi's turbo-charged engine lets off a huge roar and I swear I can see sparks come out of the exhaust pipe as the beetroot-coloured numbskull swerves his car into the oncoming lane to attempt a high-speed overtaking manoeuvre. If only it were that easy.

The BMW engine has by now also roared to life and is now screaming down the tarmac at a significantly increased speed. I'm guessing in excess of 220. Now we have two geniuses hurtling down a major highway at highly, highly illegal speeds, one of them facing oncoming traffic. All because the brain surgeon in the Beemer refuses to be overtaken by the nuclear physicist in the Audi. Who needs *Grand Theft Auto* when you can get free entertainment on the N1 on the way to Cape Town? My entrepreneurial wife quickly offers me 3:1 odds that we'd soon be seeing brain cells and macerated pancreas spread across the tarmac. The two penis-heads are still flying abreast even though there's a vehicle coming from the opposite side with furiously flicking lights. I guess it's a question of who wants it more. Joburg to Cape Town in a new six-hour land-speed record or testicular shards strewn all over the highway – whichever comes first. The clearly gonadless wimp coming from the opposite end chickens out at the last second and swerves onto the shoulder of the road. The inferno is averted and the credits roll when the Audi finally manages to overtake the Beemer. Even though I have won the wager, I curse our rotten luck. The balls of flames would have been an awesome spectacle.

This is the story of driving on South African roads. One of my everyday mottos is "Living is better than bleeding to death in a pool of my own bodily fluids". I know. You might not think so, after reading how I was operating a vehicle travelling at 140km/h. But stop changing the subject. You're missing the point. The point is that the *other* guys in the German sedans are idiots. Please try to keep up. As a matter of fact, each time anybody does anything I wouldn't do, I know they're not too bright. This seems to be the most pervasive attitude on our roads. In the South

African context, driving is that activity where an individual operates a combustible-engine-propelled vehicle for the express purpose of leaving no doubt in anyone's mind that they are superior and everyone else is a zit on a mosquito's ass.

It always amazes me how a country that scaled the heights of pragmatism displayed during our transition from the dark time could spawn the *Homo erecti* who drive alongside me everyday. Everybody is the prosecutor, judge and jury of everybody else's driving. And we all have theories why the idiot from this morning's drive just drifted into our lane without indicating. We forsake all the cause-and-effect laws that govern the rest of our universe. After we slam on the brakes, hitting our heads on the dashboard (because buckling up is for wussies), we immediately pull a stunt of our own just so we can drive abreast of the idiot to give him a really long look and then exclaim, "Yep! How did I know it was a white woman?"

Deep down in places we don't talk about we all have a driver-grading system. And we can back up our grading systems, too, even if it means invoking the spirit of Charles Darwin as we go about it. By show of hands, who has heard this one before? "It is a scientific fact that black people drive the way they do because they have impaired depth perception" – just before the embarrassed Radio 702 deejay cuts off his latest caller. What is even more impressive is the realisation that the geneticist making this assertion is probably Gert the auto mechanic from Skukuza who dropped out of school when his folks realised that Grade 8 Biology was busting his chops. But before you draw up your placards and march to the Skukuza town square, how different are you really from Gert? I know I'm not. Allow me to explain.

I am of the opinion that the reason we South Africans kill and maim each other on our roads worse than any other nation is because we're crap at maths and physics. Every survey about the appalling levels of basic numeracy in our nation seems to support my assertion. As a result, we don't seem to understand some pretty elementary concepts about driving. My pet obsession about the driving on South African roads is the lack of understanding of what seems to me a simple observation: most accidents are the result of a disturbance to the flow of traffic. This observation is not at all at loggerheads with Superintendent Wayne Minnaar's daily television "duh" assertion that "90 per cent of all accidents are preceded by a traffic violation". That's like triumphantly announcing that most conceptions are preceded by bloodcurdling screams of ecstasy. But seriously, consider my breakthrough observation. If everybody drove their vehicles in such a way as to avoid disturbing the flow of traffic, what would be the likelihood of accidents happening? Simple maths and physics dictates that if two cars are travelling in the same direction, at the same velocity, they will never make contact. Somebody call the Nobel Physics committee. These pearls of physics wisdom cannot go unrewarded. Of course, ants, that lower life form, figured this out 200 million years ago. Just watch a colony of ants file towards a crumb of bread.

Now imagine this daily scenario. You are on the two-lane R21 North from OR Tambo International Airport headed for Pretoria. For kicks, imagine that the time is 6.15am and you are trying to make it to a 7.30am appointment on the nation's capital's Pretorius Street. As you drive past the Pomona Road off-ramp, everything is going according to the way the Almighty intended it. Traffic on the left lane is flowing at an average speed of 120km/h. The average speed on the right lane is a brisk but fair 150km/h. The country's speed limits are being stretched to breaking point, naturally, but everybody is happy. No-one's shredded rectum is adorning the sparse highveld shrubbery on either side of the R21.

Enter prosecutor, judge, jury and executioner number one. Yep, the sanctimonious prick in the white Corolla happily whistling to riveting Classic FM tunes at a politically correct 110km/h in the right lane – for no plausible reason other than the fact that he can, and "after all, the speed limit is 120km/h if you care to know". Of course it is only a matter of time before the brain-damaged nitwits bearing down on him at 150 will throw themselves into the left lane to overtake him on the inside. And now you have two sets of cars in the left lane; the law-abiding citizens doing 120 and the criminally insane doing 150. These are just the ingredients necessary to get a jolly ol' inferno on the R21 at 6.15am. By the time the tardy birds get there at 7am, the road is backed up all the way to the East Rand Mall as the poor overweight Metro Police try to pick up the various bits of brain matter hanging from the early-morning blades of grass.

This is my own personal peeve about the way we drive. Believe me when I say that I truly understand the intellectual bankruptcy of driving faster than designated speeds. Elementary physics dictates that the higher the velocity, the more likely one is to soak in a pool of one's blood. I have always taken that for granted. But consider the fact that your average 1,600cc vehicle has a top speed of around 240km/h. They come that way. And that the maximum legal speed on South African roads is half that. Yet the number of times the CEO of GM South Africa has been bundled into a black Golf V belonging to the no-longer-existant Scorpions has been kept to a minimum despite the new Corsa Sport's top speed of 260km/h.

I'm sorry but that's just asking for it. As long as there are cars designed to reach exceptionally high speeds, there will be sporadic sightings of radio deejays doing exceptionally high speeds on public roads. Ditto overfed perpetually angry former cabinet ministers. And they will spread their arms and splutter, "Sorry, this luxury German sedan is so comfortable I did not realise I was doing 257km/h." Expecting humans not to exceed the piddly 120km/h speed limit when their cars are designed to reach 250km/h in a heartbeat is not realistic. That's like dropping your kid off at the Michael Jackson Nursery School and being surprised when "incidents" occur. And in the unlikely event that I am not clear on this, I don't condone speeding. Speeding is a dangerous and retarded practice. I'm just saying it is to be expected. It's human nature.

But the speedsters are not on trial today. The morons crawling in the right lane are. And I'm calling it the "right lane" consciously. That's because it is not the "fast lane". Part of the problem with South Africa is that we do not call things by their proper names. We call turn signals "indicators", which is why we only touch them to indicate to the people behind us that we have already turned. Maybe if we called it a turn signal, we would use it to signal our intention to turn into the next lane. And I often get the distinct impression that some people believe that driving in the "fast lane" automatically makes their vehicles go faster. This is a much more serious possibility than you might think. Because how many times have you seen someone driving in the right lane, completely oblivious to the fact that the cars in the left lane are speeding past him? Or seen a 22-metre truck hurl itself onto the right lane at an impressive 58km/h in order to overtake his counterpart who is struggling along at a snail's pace of 55 km/h on the N3 to Durban? And then the rest of you have to form an uhuru election queue behind him because this daring feat takes him 17 minutes.

But enough with the pontificating. I have my own driving retardations: idiocies such as operating a vehicle while sending a text message with one hand, reaching out for a beer in the cubby-hole with the other hand and steering with my knees while approaching Gillooly's Interchange during peak hour. And with that, we have reached a point in this rant where I must regale you with my grading system for the worst drivers on South African roads according to Ndumiso Ngcobo.

The first group of drivers I cannot stand are coastal-town drivers. Durban, Cape Town and Port Elizabeth are all in one clump of inadequacy. Yes, the whole lot of you. If there is salt water corroding your vehicle's panels as you read this, I'm talking about you. And I'm originally from Durban myself. I know on a personal level the depths of inadequacy that I waddled in when I first came to the city of skilled driving. If you're from Gauteng, tell me if this has ever happened to you.

You're in the right lane of Durban's M4 North trying to get to La Lucia Mall, using a map, after 4.30pm. Because the signage in that part of the world was designed for someone who has been using the route all his life, you realise too late that you are a mere 400m away from the exit you need to take. So you have to try to manoeuvre your way into the appropriate lane as quickly as possible. Watch what happens when you switch on the left turn signal and attempt to take advantage of the ten-metre gap between the cars on your left. After all, you're from the nation's financial hub, your GP plates should be leaving no-one in doubt as to your intrinsic superiority. Contributing the lion's share of the gross domestic productivity is not easy. Not only that, you've been known to squeeze into a three-metre gap at the William Nichol exit off the N1.

But not in Durban. As soon as you switch on that turn signal, that ten-metre gap instantly drops to a 30-centimetre crack. Not even the value of the Zim dollar shrinks so quickly. Now try to honk to attract the Durbanite's attention – which is the point at which you will be educated to the look I like to call the Durban Stare-ahead. People from coastal towns are quite adept at this. I have seen a perfect execution of the Durban Stare-ahead on Sea Point's Main Road as well. And it's not that people from these places are meaner. It's just a function of the fact that your average Durbanite was born in Phoenix, studied in Phoenix and Durban town, married a girl from Sea Cow Lake and works in Umhlanga. All within a 20-kilometre radius. He cannot possibly fathom why anyone would want to change lanes at this late hour. Are you out of your mind? Unless you're a taxi driver willing to make your point by bending your fender, there's no chance you will ever get into that gap. Indeed, if you love your car you might have to drive all the way to Mt Edgecombe before you can turn around.

Another road user I cannot stand is actually two road users: the elderly white couple. Oh, they piss me off. Especially if the white elderly female is behind the steering wheel because the George Burns lookalike in the passenger seat has a hearing aid sticking out of his ear. To begin with, Estelle Getty over there has the self-assuredness of someone who has been behind the wheel of a car since 1957 and no grandson of John the gardener is going to teach her how to drive. So you will have to toast patiently in the sun for a good 22 minutes (minimum) while she executes a complicated seven-point manoeuvre in her 1988 Honda Ballade just to get out of a parking bay at the mall. Twenty-two minutes is a sitcom episode, damn it!

And then there's the elderly black man in a powder-blue 1973 Toyota Hilux bakkie with 200 chickens inside a wire-mesh enclosure and three goats at the back. I can't stand this road user! Driving behind the elderly black man with the Stone Age bakkie makes one wonder at Piet Koornhof's wisdom in allowing the Department of Bantu Affairs to issue the bar-coded IDs that made it possible for the old man to get a driver's licence. A gentle curve on the road will have everybody behind him come to a virtual dead stop because he insists on taking the bend no faster than 5km/h.

About the only drivers I can stand are young white males and young black males. And that's mostly because I have learnt that any outward display of displeasure at the antics of these two groups is a story that ends badly. It's a story that ends with a short podgy man using his huge head as the last line of defence against blows thrown with serious venom. It's the type of ending that invokes my early Christian tendencies – I just turn the other cheek. That's because this group is a victim of testosterone. Look at the models of cars this group prefers. They mostly have vehicles that have a phallic theme. The next time you see angry Mark in a Subaru, take a closer look at the shape of his car. It's just an extension of his penis. While you think he's driving, he's not. He's actually parting the sea of cement with his huge member. Standing in his way is a bad, bad idea.

At this juncture, Gert from Skukuza and I would like to invite you to draw up your own grading system of moronic drivers. You know it's inside your head. Some people can't stand egotistical Beemer drivers, others can't stand Corsa Lite drivers with small-car syndrome. Just pick a group of drivers and all of us can go on our merry way honking and calling each other idiots. It's great fun.

Meanwhile, I have a friend called Maswazi, who often gets a faraway look in his eye as he fantasises about what he would do if he won the R20-million jackpot in the Lotto. He tells me he'd quit his job and join the Johannesburg Metro Police to show them a thing or two about policing the roads. When he gets started about what he'd get up to, there is a fire in that glint of his more ferocious than anything the Tsitsikamma Forest has ever witnessed. He explains that he'd spend his days just driving around in an unmarked vehicle. Motorists always find a deep-seated respect for the law in the presence of a vehicle with JMPD emblazoned on its side, so he'd take the incognito route looking for dowdy Estelle Getty lookalikes to pull over for hogging the right lane, knocking them on the forehead with his knuckles and asking, "Which part of 70km/h makes you believe you belong in this lane, huh?" He'd give out R3,000 fines the same way Janet Jackson gives out her titties to dairy-deficient fans – irrespective of transgressions. He'd arrest any motorist on the spot if they complained that three grand for changing lanes without signalling was too steep, and add "Interfering with an officer's duty" to their charge sheet. Poor Maswazi always sighs deeply when he fantasises about taxi drivers. He says he'd be completely unreasonable with this bunch. He'd pull over taxis willy-nilly during peak hour and make the drivers chant the affirmation "The yellow line shall not be crossed at any point" a thousand times until peak-hour traffic subsided. When taxi drivers inevitably blockaded the Johannesburg CBD and toyi-toyi'd to the Metro Department offices, he says he'd occupy a building across the street and use live ammunition on them as if he were an ANC bodyguard during the Shell House days. Or a Metro Policeman on strike…

Before I go completely off the deep end, let me reel myself in. In the interests of monotonous repetition I need to reiterate the fact that I think the human brain is perhaps the most consistent machine when it comes to regular malfunctioning. Trust thy brain at thine own risk. Most people I know get into their cars for the sole purpose of getting from point A to point B. A not-so-silent minority drives to prove that their penis is bigger than Mark's in the Subaru. Since fathering Ntobeko, my first son, my attitude to driving has changed. Ntobeko's birth cleared my mind of the need to prove anything to anybody. Nowadays I drive for one purpose and one purpose only. I drive to not die. This is when I'm not driving at 140km/h with my baby in the back.

I think that we have lost too many people who were adding value to our society purely because they didn't have the common sense to buckle up as they went about pushing their over-powered vehicles to the limit. That's because their brains were malfunctioning. They have a way of doing that.

Ask a fruit fly whether it would like to be stuffed into a matchbox and thrown from table height without being strapped down first. Its answer will be, "Where's the strap?"

Is It Coz I'm Black?

The Hunchback Of Howard College

'm a coward. I fear everybody. I am afraid of virtually every demographic grouping in this country.

I fear, for example, the righteous indignation of white females. Have you ever had an altercation with a white female? Only white females will furiously castigate you with, "Well, I'm sorry but that's just unacceptable and *rude!*" (pronounced "rooowd") and think they sure told you. That's a special kind of anger. Black women, meanwhile, will cuss you, your mother and your father, and question the length of some of your appendages. And I fear Indian females, too, because they are always one argument away from putting a curse on your ass. "I hope God blesses you," you might hear – and when you do, you're doomed. You best believe that the next time you see an individual in a surgical ward with a penis growing out of his ear, that guy had a run-in with an Indian female. Then, just to prove I'm not too sexist, I also fear black men because black men will beat you up and leave you with a speech impediment just because you looked at them funny.

Take a close look at any segment of our population and there'll be something to quiver at – but it's the angry white male that I fear more than anybody else.

The angry white male, or AWM if you will, has an intense rage that took me years to understand. I used to recoil from the TV set each time a furious Tony Leon appeared with his characteristic scowl, smouldering eyes and volcanic eruptions spewing forth from his lips. Tony Leon pisses all over "Terror" Lekota in the anger stakes, I reckon – and Terror is one angry dude. I personally heaved a huge sigh of relief when Livid Tony got tired of pissing against the wind trying to win against the ANC. Of course, he passed on the baton of rage to that woman with the face of a Bulgarian weightlifter who scares the living shit out of me, too. But at least she wears a brassiere and has been known to dabble in Botox treatments.

My introduction to the world of white-male anger came during my first year at the (then) University of Natal in Durban, thanks to a super-intelligent, sophisticated and suave biology lecturer. I like to call him Dr Hunchback for reasons that I'll refrain from going into. (Just trust me that the name is appropriate, in the same spirit that we were meant to trust Thabo Mbeki on the Jackie Selebi matter…) Dr Hunchback was, if my whisky-compromised recollection serves me, a molecular biologist or geneticist of sorts. I could be wrong, though, so let's just say he was a white-coat-clad nerd with many letters after his name.

There are many compelling reasons for my appalling academic record in that institution of higher learning. They include my pathological laziness, which led to me spending my afternoons watching double features at the Avalon Raj cinema on Victoria Street, and my tireless hunt for females with receptive vajayjays (to borrow a word from the incredible Oprah Winfrey). But part of the reason for my impressive consistency in obtaining low scores in examinations was the attitude of the mostly white-male lecturers. During the first leg of my first year of studies at this previously all-white university I had an experience that sums up the attitude I'm referring to.

It was a Monday afternoon, biology practical. For the benefit of the non-scientifically minded reading this, biology practicals are those exercises where students spend three hours slicing open a rat for the purpose of exposing its pancreas and testicles and whatnot. Biology lecturers get off on that sort of thing and may or may not be known to experience orgasms at the sight of a perfectly carved-up rodent cadaver. Generations of biology students have been subjected to this sadistic orgy of pointless violence. And just so that biology professors may possess a record of the students' butchering skills to beat off to later, students are then encouraged to draw diagrams of the sliced-up little beasts.

My laboratory partner was a dude with a girly name who remains a friend of mine until this very day. If anybody is interested, I did not choose to be his partner; the lab technician was responsible for pairing the students. I presume that when he pulled the names out from a hat, it just so happened that I was paired with one of only three black gentlemen out of a class of more than 40. These coincidences happen. In any case, Dr Hunchback was moving stealthily in between the work stations surveying the rodent carcasses on butcher foil paper for his own titillation. At

The Hunchback Of Howard College

some point he came up behind my partner and me to have a look at our drawings.

"Impressive drawings, young men," he declared, "considering the fact that black people cannot see in more than two dimensions."

Gulp. What?

"Oh no, don't look so surprised. It's a scientific fact. It has to do with the fact that, anatomically speaking, black people's brains have larger fissures between the lobes."

Double gulp. Burning temples.

The hunchback then proceeded to elucidate the significance of the space between brain hemispheres and depth perception. He even volunteered the fact that if we were to study cave drawings of the Bushmen, we would be hard-pressed to find three-dimensional drawings. As he regaled us with this irrefutable scientific logic, his perpetually moist upper lip quivered and his teeth were bared in a cruel and vicious snarl. I realised then that the man who was talking to us had a deep, deep rage boiling inside of him. Had it not been for the fact that I had taken a whizz before the practical session, my boxers would likely have been soaked by this stage. That's how terrified I was. My friend with the girly name giggled nervously. I looked at him and realised that he did indeed have two bumps on his forehead that created an illusion of an accentuated fissure between his brain lobes. So I remained open-minded – no pun intended – to the possibility that this great intellectual giant standing over my shoulder was indeed correct about this. After all, he had years of experience in the field of scientific fact-gathering.

Two years later, I was asked to leave the faculty on grounds of inadequate academic progression. I can't imagine why obtaining an average of 47 per cent in that time should be grounds for expulsion from university but such is life. The hunchback's parting words in my direction went something like this: "If all else fails – and it's currently pointing strongly in that direction – take comfort in the knowledge that you probably didn't belong here in any case. It's not your fault. But your grasp of the English language is good. You will do relatively well on the other side of campus"

– Humanities – "where most of your people are."

You will be forgiven for asking yourself how old I am because this sounds like something somebody might have said in the early 1960s. No, the year was 1989 and that great liberating shiny-top, FW de Klerk, had already made huge strides by declaring that the Bantus could swim on North Beach.

So I went elsewhere. My friend with the girly name stuck it out. He is now the Head of Operations in a food-ingredient-manufacturing multinational after years of distinguishing himself in the manufacturing sector. Not bad for a man with no depth perception. And just to reassure you, I also eventually managed to obtain a qualification in the sciences.

Most people believe that white-male anger stems from rabid racism. I may, admittedly, be as ignorant as they come but that just doesn't ring true. Of course, I'm not saying white males are impervious to racism; if anything, they are the one group that has the *cojones* to do something about their particular prejudices – unlike the rest of us cowardly racist pigs. But I think that aspect of the white male is under control. Well, most of the time anyway.

I have never been convinced that one group of people is more afflicted by the chronic racism ailment than another. Bob Marley believed that racism was an actual disease that needed either to be cured or surgically removed. I agree completely with him about it being a pathological condition. Where I think the ganja started messing with Bob's brain is when he started talking about magic remedies. I think racism is a disease without a cure in the mould of diabetes, AIDS and the love of hip-hop music. And just like those other chronic ailments, the best approach to racism is to manage it through lifestyle choices.

Other (highly immature) people believe that white-male anger comes from the same place that gives rise to a spectacular lack of rhythmic coordination. If you're one of those people, I have two words for you: grow the eff up. Admittedly, most white okes I know dance like a mummy in a full body cast who has just stepped on a termite colony, but I'm afraid that does not satisfy root-cause analysis criteria. On, then, to what I believe is the problem…

I think white-male anger comes from their innate knowledge that white men should be running the world. And white men are not necessarily running the world quite to their satisfaction. Please allow me the latitude to expand on my retarded theory.

Centuries ago white males skulked around peacefully in European caves hunting moose, clubbing their women over the head to make babies, calling each other "dude" and saying stuff like "totally rockers" and "awesome". (The Africans, Asians, native Americans and Australians were doing exactly the same, by the way. Except that "rockers" thing: that's an exclusive white-male thing.) Then they got a bit sophisticated, invented the wheel and stuff, and took to calling themselves Goths or some other cool rock-band-type name. But their peaceful existence was interrupted by those pesky Moors, who I've discussed at length already in chapter 7. Aggressive black North African hordes that they were, they invaded Europe and essentially took over the entire place, pillaging, plundering the sparse resources and pissing in the drinking water. Naturally, the white guys were quite perturbed by this development. But after a while they got used to the nonsense – even the pissing-in-the-water thing.

Things reached tipping point, however, when the Moors got more belligerent and started making unreasonable demands. One of these was that the Goths had to send a hundred Gothic virgins per annum to the Moorish leaders for use in their harems. A harem is essentially the same as King Zwelithini's *isigodlo*, the place where His Majesty keeps his many women. The white dudes reluctantly complied for a few decades but this was the last straw because, you see, the Moors were hung like the stallions they rode. The virgins had a tough time. So then the Goths gathered at Kliptown in downtown Gothic Soweto, wrote the original Freedom Charter and waged a liberation struggle that culminated in a famous victory for the rock 'n' roll guys, with hundreds of thousands of Moors lying in pools of their own blood. Bear with me, I'm going somewhere with this.

In the ensuing centuries the white dudes then went about giving the brown world a taste of their own medicine. They used the Chinese alchemist monk invention, gunpowder, to make many, many guns. The Chinese were otherwise preoccupied with drinking the stuff in search of the elixir of immortality to get closer to Tao – or something like that. I wonder if the Chinese appreciated the irony when the Gothic dudes from that aggressive island in the Atlantic invaded and defeated them in that war over the 19th-century drug trade using their own invention. I bet they wished they had focused more on developing guns and gunpowder rather than developing their opium habits and dying painful diarrhoeic deaths. In any case, the white guys, armed with their thunder guns, then descended upon the rest of the world, including these parts, and spent a few centuries digging big holes in the ground, trying to turn Africa into Europe and putting natives in their place. It was a roaring success for the most part. I mean, I'm writing this in one of those Gothic dialects, aren't I?

And this, I believe, is the gist of the source of modern white-male anger: having their backs against the wall when they have the glorious history that they have. Who can argue against the fact that the last couple of centuries have belonged to the white male, after all? Anyone? To bastardise Tony Montana from *Scarface*: the world is *theirs*! Well, until the belligerence of their Moorish forefathers started rearing its ugly head again and the natives started rebelling. More Freedom Charters and things followed, finally culminating in 27 April 1994 when the last of the natives made an uncomfortable deal with the white dudes. The white okes were not really vanquished in the classical sense of being defeated – like those bleeding Moors. Everything was negotiated.

To quote an AWM friend of mine: "I cannot get over the fact that every time I look around me, I'm reminded that white males like myself built all of this." Before everybody descends upon me like hobos on a soup kitchen and starts quoting exotic Kara Heritage-esque literature to me, I'm well aware that the fact that white men built everything around us is in dispute. Humour me and consider this whole situation from the AWM's perspective. After all, popular history has painstakingly recorded how the spawn of the Goths went around the world inventing stuff and popularising inventions to every corner of the world. They brought everybody modern science, technology, aviation, the World Wide Web, chewing gum and Crocs. (Where would we be today, for example, if the internet had not brought us the Big Black Booty website?)

This is where I get to ask you, assuming you're a non-AWM, an important question. If you were a white male, wouldn't you be right royally furious too with being perpetually pushed to the margins by a bunch of people who don't even have the balls to bludgeon you to death with a blunt tomahawk before assuming power? I mean, that's the least you should do if you're serious about running shit. Can you imagine the Moors or Cecil John Rhodes signing a negotiated settlement and living side by side with the presumably vanquished? What retarded nonsense is this? Wouldn't it really irritate you too to see people using the AWM-invented internet to attack you before they get into their AWM-invented Hummers to drive to their homes and guzzle AWM-invented Scotch to plot the marginalisation of the same said AWMs? To clarify my point, allow me to adapt a quote from that legend of fiction Colonel Nathan Jessup from *A Few God Men*: "I have neither the time nor the inclination to explain myself to a man who drives the Hummer I invented, drinks the Johnny Walker I distilled and then questions the manner in which I provide them. I would rather you just said 'thank you', got on your knees to fellate me, ate your piss-spiked food and went on your way."

Oh, I'm shit-scared of the AWM. And I'm not talking about your regular white guy here. You know that regular white guy, surely? Peaceful, sedate and reasonable – like Van Zyl Slabbert or Jeremy Cronin. No, I'm talking about the livid white guy with veins popping out of his forehead because you drove into the parking bay he was eyeing from 100 metres away. That's the white guy who makes me shake in my boots; the guy who starts every sentence with the words, "Listen here, you poes…" I'm talking about the guy who looks like Theunis Botha from the DA. It must take a lot of anger to maintain that moustache.

And don't you just love how AWMs are simply impervious to being taken on a guilt trip about the whole apartheid and colonialism thing? White women are putty in my hands when I'm on my best "blame whitey" trip. We darkies are very good at this. I've had two white female bosses before and used the white-guilt thing to great effect, especially around performance-appraisal time:

> *White Female:* I am not impressed. Your work is shoddy and your attention to detail is shocking…
> *Me:* Apartheid.
> *WF:* What?
> *Me:* You'd struggle with attention to detail, too, if you were the product of Bantu Education.
> *WF* [tearfully]: You poor thing. How about a 50 per cent raise and the opportunity to bury your head in my cleavage on demand as reparation?

I personally think we let whiteys off the hook way too quickly when it comes to this sort of thing. I mean, these okes gave us an education system that forced every black person to recite a piece of "poetic" nothingness called *Muskiete Jag*. The fact that generations of black people can repeat this foolishness off by heart pisses the smouldering hell out of me:

> *Jou vabond, wag ek sal jou kry*
> *Van jou sal net 'n bloedkol bly*
> *Hier op my kammer mure…*

See what I mean? This was a crime against humanity. It's the type of thing we should have TRCed or at least used as a bargaining tool to negotiate five more percentage points in employment-equity quotas. But, unlike white women, the AWM is generally quite unfazed by this sort of thing.

This brings me to another feature of white males that always amazes me. I think white males lack the "ignorance" gene. Allow that one to simmer a little bit. I am 36 years old and I am reasonably confident that I have never heard a white male say "I don't know" followed by a full stop. I'll tell you what I have heard them say: "I don't know really, but what I think is happening is…" – followed by a ten-minute theory on that which they have already claimed not to know.

When I worked in a food-manufacturing plant as an R&D assistant manager, I once walked into the process-engineering department to ask a technical question about the process flow during a manufacturing trial. The process engineer in charge of the area was, at that moment, on the phone, so I waited. His colleague, an AWM, promptly broke into a lengthy, unsolicited lecture on the process flow in that area, the exact routing of the pipes, the actuation mechanism of every valve and the precise location of every tank. About five minutes into the riveting explanation, the bloke I had originally come to see interrupted the conversation with one word: "Rubbish". He then produced a process-flow diagram from his desk and repudiated everything the AWM had said. He was right, too. But that's not the point.

Everybody is right and wrong at some point. The point is that this dude gave me his hallucinatory crap with absolute confidence, without even a blink. The fact that it never occurred to him once that he could be talking right out of his rectum really struck home for me. I like that about AWMs. The ability to bullshit confidently is an underrated skill in my book. I wish I had it. After all, you cannot create the system of apartheid while continuously second-guessing yourself. You don't build empires that way. It is this kind of unwavering self-belief in your correctness that gives a person the audacity to wipe entire civilisations off the face of the earth, to dig really big holes in the ground and send conquered minions down into the belly of the earth to retrieve shiny metals, and to generally create lasting legacies. I wouldn't be able to do it, wake up the following morning and have a large continental breakfast. I know what I have: weak-bellyitis.

When all is said and done, I hope that my incoherent rant serves the purpose of making everybody understand the AWM a little better. I shall conclude with a passage from a dead AWM, who was known for writing the occasional play and speaking some wisdom:

If we shadows have offended,
Think but this, and all is mended:
That you have but slumber'd here
While these visions did appear.
And this weak and idle theme,
No more yielding but a dream,
Gentles, do not reprehend.
If you pardon, we will mend.

Is It Coz I'm Black?

The Church Of Thirst And The Beard

I remember the worst interview I ever saw on TV. Considering that I have probably watched a few thousand television interviews in my life, this is quite a statement. Evander Holyfield had just finished beating up on one "Iron" Mike Tyson in their first match-up, in November 1996. This is not to be confused with their second fight, during which Tyson got a little peckish and snacked on Holyfield's ear. Boxing commentator and analyst Freddie Pacheco steps up to Evander for a post-fight interview, and the interview goes along these lines:

> *Freddie Pacheco:* I gotta say that was the biggest surprise in boxing I've ever had.
> *Evander Holyfield:* Well, I give glory to God and for everybody to know that you cannot choose against God. You can choose against me anytime but when God's involved, Jesus is alive and… I thank God…
> *FP:* Why did you guarantee your victory with such assurance?
> *EH:* Coz anybody who puts God up there… My God is the only true God and everything must bow to God.
> *FP:* Okay, apart from religion because I hope God is here for all of us. Let's get off that and let's get back to boxing. How did you fight such a brilliant fight?
> *EH:* I've lived by the Spirit of God. I told everybody that whatever the Spirit leads me to do I would do…

And this is what happened throughout the entire interview. The interviewer tried his darndest to get Evander to talk about the tactics he used to take on and defeat one of the most-feared men in boxing history but all Evander wanted to talk about was how his superior God led him to victory. It made for seriously irritating TV because nobody watching was interested in how that gaseous entity that sometimes goes by the pseudonym Spirit influenced Evander's impressive left hooks and right uppercuts. And with that, let's take a detour.

I am also an irrational believer in God. Not that I think there's any other kind of believer in God. And just to stir the hornet's nest a little, I don't

144   *Is It Coz I'm Black?*

think that anyone who denies God's existence comes from a position of superior rationality either. Yes, I said it: atheists are an irrational bunch too. Their irrationality is, in my opinion, at a similar level to that of Evander Holyfield when it comes to Godly matters.

In fact, the only bunch with a relatively rational stance when it comes to God matters is those wishy-washy, fence-sitting bet-hedgers who call themselves agnostics. I like to sum up the agnostics' view with the classic, "I'm not saying God doesn't exist, I'm just saying I haven't seen Him." (Of course, the agnostics out there wouldn't use a capital letter "G" if they were representing themselves.) Having said that, agnostics are the only people who are neither moved by the Spirit nor make quantum leaps in logic from a lack of evidence to the nonexistence of God. Learned theologians with seventeen PhDs would probably crush me like a car flattening a chameleon trying to cross a highway for the bankruptcy of my conclusions – especially if they practise the more intellectual palatable form of theology called contextual theology – but this is what I'm going with.

Atheists always charge that God is simply a figment of the weak human brain. In other words, God is a creation of believers. Funnily enough, if atheists are right, then atheists are the creation of believers' weak brains, too. After all, if believers hadn't created God, there wouldn't be any atheists around. Richard Dawkins, the author of *The God Delusion*, might have had to settle for a book titled *The Tooth-Fairy Delusion* instead. And let's agree that this would have been a pretty crappy book. Thank God for those irrational believers.

The reason I make this point is because nothing riles up atheists like the type of tautological argument I've just made. It usually sends them into a frothing-at-the-mouth rage, which always reminds me of those TV evangelists in full cry. Ironic, no?

I cannot pinpoint the exact moment when I was first introduced to the concept of God. I cannot even credit the stout women with moustaches who instructed me in the catechism with this information. The concept of God is just one of those things I seem to have always known, like the sky, the oceans and Mick Jagger. This always begs the question of whether I came to the vague, fuzzy "knowledge" that God exists on my own or whether it was brainwashed into me. It seems to me quite a critical thing, this. Especially considering that even before the days of travel and global communication, virtually all the tribes of the world came to a series of independent conclusions that God exists.

And it seems that, irrespective of where people developed their God concept, it became very important to define the God concept. Some people described him as a supernatural "being", not too dissimilar to people. That's what I was told when I was small: that we are made in God's image. I find that I am struggling more and more with this concept. The idea of a God with emotions who gets angry, loves, punishes and gets jealous doesn't sound right. That sounds like a whole lot of frailty to me – and that doesn't make me comfortable. I mean, could He get so angry he'd instruct Jupiter to nudge the southernmost tip of Africa? Plus, where does it stop with a God like us? Does he approve of beer? Weed? It seems to me that a God wouldn't bother with such minor detail. Plus, I have a problem with the inherent arrogance this betrays. Why us? Why not bats or hyenas? Or Smurfs? I think it's the height of delusions of grandeur. If I had to define God, I'd probably want an extremely inert, impermeable God.

I was born and grew up in house number A662 in an insignificant little township northwest of Durban, called Mpumalanga. No need to be silly now, I wasn't born in the actual matchbox itself. There was no involvement of a one-eyed toothless woman with seven layers of shawls and boiling water in a 20-litre paint can next to a stack of towels. I just mean that when my mom left for the hospital, she left from house A662. I have often hypothesised that if I had been born in number 36 Ghatkopar Road in Mumbai and my name was Rajkumar Singh, there is a high likelihood that I would be practising a different brand of irrational God worship. I always take it for granted that I would consider anyone stuffing their faces with beef sausages as some kind of primitive heathen. And if I'd been born Malachi Benjamin in Tel Aviv, I'd probably have the same aversion to swine munchers. Whenever I have put this submission to fellow irrational believers, they have tended to get really upset with my suggestion that their Jesus love has got more than just a hint of "accident of birth" about it. Colourful characterisations such as "devil worshipper" might even have been bandied about from time to time. But I was born with a hormonal imbalance that makes me derive pleasure from having insults hurled at me so I don't really mind.

My own unwavering spirituality is founded upon a solid pragmatism. In my infinite pragmatism, I don't believe in taking unnecessary chances. My solid faith is based on a couple of what-if questions. What if there really *is* a place called hell after we die? What if there really *will* be a Second Coming and a Judgment Day? I have serious problems with things scratching against surfaces, such as nails on a chalkboard and whatnot; I always get that awful reverberation in my teeth. So when the holy men start describing that whole Hell option, what with the graphic "wailing and gnashing of teeth" reference, I get nervous. Imagine your teeth gnashing for an eternity. Nothing good could possibly come of that. I fear the possibility of gnashing of teeth so badly that I'm just not willing to take the odds, however good, that the dude who wrote the Book of Revelations was a pothead – or Stephen King's forefather.

This is all to say that I'd hate to be chilling with other men of thirst, sipping on some amber liquids, only for the skies to open and me to realise that, oops, the guys in shiny robes were right! I sure wouldn't want to be an atheist at that moment. Plus I imagine things would work out such that there wouldn't be enough time to quickly grab a jackhammer and knock out one's teeth. You know, to circumvent the whole gnashing-of-teeth scenario. I'm sorry, that's a chance I'm not willing to take. (But I imagine that a sizeable portion of the Cape Flats population wouldn't worry about such details. Call it a hunch.)

As a result, I try my damndest to live a relatively evil-free life. I do not want to jinx my chances of avoiding the teeth-gnashing place by lying here so I'll admit it: I'm failing miserably so far. My midterm report card for how I have lived my life so far would probably look like this:

Subject	Marks (%)	Symbol	Teacher comments
Wrath	32*	F	Poor effort. You need to stop being such an angry little twerp.
Sloth	21*	G	You gotta get off your fat arse and do stuff. It's that simple.
Greed	45*	E	Stop chasing after money. Stop it! Take this book, for instance. Was it really necessary?
Gluttony	61	C	Your strong point. Still, lay off those little cocktail sausages.
Envy	34*	F	Not too bad. Ogling thy brother's wife's legs is dragging you down.
Aggregate	39	F	You might be doing slightly better than the rest – still, you're on your way to teeth gnashing.

I have recently concluded that I cannot afford to be in this situation. Something's gotta give. If not for my own escape from the eternal inferno in hell, then I need to improve my scores for the greater good of mankind.

In the end it doesn't matter whether or not there is really a place called hell where people grind their teeth to powder. I believe that the true value of religion is that it makes people good – good to themselves and good to others. To whomever just thought to themselves, "The Crusades", please let's not change the subject. I have been a recipient of great generosity from religious people all my life. Even the high school I went to was run by a bunch of nuns who were getting paid exactly nothing to give me a quality education. That is a fact. Their faith yielded that tangible positive result. Whether or not there really is a heaven is something a few of them will have found out, having now passed on – just like the rest of us will find out when we die.

But let's backtrack to that Crusades issue for a second. If religion is such a great thing, then why is there also so much hatred, so much strife, so much violence and so much tension between people of different faiths? From what I can see, at the most basic level all major religions have common threads. There is agreement on some core issues:

- There is a higher power in existence. Jehovah, Allah, Yahweh, Jah, Buddha, Vishnu – that's just detail.
- The higher power always manifests itself in human form at some point. (Never in insect form. Dung beetles, for instance, are out of the higher-power-manifestation loop.)
- The higher-power-human manifestation comes from the Asian continent and is generally male.
- The higher-power-human manifestation generally tends to keep a full beard and is quite partial to flowing robes and/or frocks.

With so much in common, one has to wonder what all the fighting and name-calling is about. You'd think that two men from different religions would talk to each other across the fence in very cordial terms. You see, truly religious men tend to model themselves after the higher-power-human manifestations even to this day. So they're supposed to be pretty sympathetic to each other's lot in life.

Bearded Male I: You with the nice robe, what are you up to?
Bearded Male II: Nothing much. I just finished combing my beard.
BM I: And what a lovely beard it is. Pity about the heat. My own beard gets really hot and itchy in this weather.
BM II: I know. If we were not such pious men we might be grumpy, get

generally very irritable and start unnecessary wars against each other.
BM I: You're quite right. But such behaviour would make us no better than dung beetles.
BM II: True. You are rather higher-powerish, I must say. Go well, neighbour.

Scene fades with them in a passionate, religious embrace, beards glistening in the Mediterranean sun.

Of course such a scene could only happen in Utopia. Sadly, in the real world things are different. I have never been able to understand the tension between the different sub-categories of believers. That animosity has always just blown my mind. What seems to be the problem here? I haven't been able to think of anything other than a simple case of Teacher's Pet syndrome.

Perhaps – and this is just a thought – it's worth considering that our belief systems are pretty difficult to swallow for someone who didn't grow up with them. Perhaps, while you giggle privately at the irrationality of a man who believes that God lives inside Bessie the cow or even a blue-spotted skunk, it might be worth remembering that he probably has a good laugh at your belief that 2,000 years ago a pious woman prayed so hard that God took it upon Himself to knock her up. Without knocking her up. To someone from Islamabad, that's how crazy the concept of Immaculate Conception sounds. It sounded crazy to me, too, until I spent hundreds of hours at catechism. And then those other pious women with Mary-envy drilled it into my head that if I didn't believe these stories literally I would spend an eternity being cornholed by well-hung devils – in conjunction with all the wailing and gnashing of teeth. It did wonders for my faith.

I think it's fair to say that we can all make a collective admission that it takes some pretty concentrated Jesus juice to swallow some of these stories literally. I mean, surfing on water without a board, dude? Why is this necessary for me to believe? Does this story enhance the fact that if we all lived a Christ-like life things would be neat? Does it really have that effect on anyone living in 2009? Somehow I doubt it, but maybe it's just me.

One of my friends is a human tub of tallow that I nicknamed The Sumo a few years back. You have to see him to understand. The Sumo and I have had extensive discussions about starting our own church. And we might have already started the church, too, if we didn't have irrational hang-ups about the repercussions of defrauding poor people on a mass scale. That does not mean the idea is completely dead. Let's just say it's still marinating in our ideas bank. But if we did forge ahead, I truly believe we'd start a pretty awesome church to rival anything there is out there. For starters, we'd have a trump card in The Sumo on account of his bodily dimensions. Just take a look at most African Pentecostal Church bishops. Yes sirree, one needs to be quite wide of girth to qualify. And trust me, The Sumo exudes "bishop". Slap a beard on him and we're in business. I can already see him in one of those curtain-net vests favoured by most denominations, staff in hand, singing the universal anthem of Pentecostal churches: "Ngizonibhevula Ngamunye Ngamunye".

We'd have to name our church carefully. I saw a church on Thema Road, KwaThema in Springs, the other day called the Republican Trinity Church of Christ in South Africa. Now that's how you name a church. Just open a newspaper, close your eyes and put your hand on a word. If it so happens that your finger lands on a story about the American elections, you might end up with Republican Trinity. I know; the name conjures up images of a Republican Trinity to me, too: Father Bush, Son Bush and Dick Cheney, the Holy Goat. It beats Church of England in South Africa hands down. This is why The Sumo and I have settled on The Three Wise Men of Thirst Full Gospel Church of Christ in Southern Africa. And there are sound reasons for this name.

For starters, "in Southern Africa" has an all-encompassing phantom-regional ring to it as opposed to the limiting "in South Africa". This would give us options. After all, there are more Bulawayan citizens in Yeoville than there are in Bulawayo. There's also the Full Gospel part of the name. That's a clever move, if I say so myself. I mean who would go to the Half

Gospel Church when the Full Gospel is right there? And then there's the "of Thirst" bit in the name just in case *The Daily Sun* reported that the bishops were seen in a watering hole. We'd shrug and say, "Yeah, so what? We are a church of thirst."

The Sumo and I would run a tight and modern church. Let's all agree that using the bishop's wife's good china to collect money during the service is an archaic Stone Age practice. No. We'll have a Mastercard and VISA sign at the gate and pass around those portable Speedpoints during the entire service. And each row will have one, too. No point in having a ten-minute window for collections. And each time The Sumo strikes a chord during his two-hour sermon, gullible pensioners would moan loudly and say "pass the ironing machine". Every member of the church would have to surrender their ATM machine card PIN as part of the registration. We'd run credit and liquidity-status checks, and reject anyone undergoing debt counselling with the quotable quote, "Jesus doesn't want losers."

We wouldn't do anything in half measures. For instance, we'd launch our church on an infomercial slot shot on location over the River Jordan. Gullible, poor domestic-worker types believe that the River Jordan is in heaven. No living person could possibly reach the River Jordan, they believe – the Bible says that's a heavenly place, after all. A lay minister in my current church went to the Holy Land once and spoke about having soaked his feet in the River Jordan; he's been known as a pathological liar since that day. So you can imagine the effect of a shot of The Sumo in a white flowing robe, full beard glistening in the Middle Eastern sun, knee-deep in River Jordan waters…

Our method for determining seniority in the church structure would be uncomplicated and transparent. Full beard length would be the criterion for choosing church elders. Of course we would have a head start over everyone else – just like the top guy in a pyramid scheme – because we'd start growing our own beards at least two years before the launch. If Willy Madisha tried to join, we'd just reject his application, ostensibly on the grounds of a certain missing R500,000. The real reason would be the threat posed by his advanced beard, of course.

In the event of any dissension within the ranks, the rules would be clear:

Beard > No beard
Full beard > Partial beard
Grey beard > Black beard

In the event of a tie in terms of the beard criteria, the flowability of the robe would be the tie-breaker. And a white robe would hold the edge over an off-white robe. If there was still any confusion, sandals would carry more weight than closed shoes. An example of how this would work:

Junior Bishop I: Like King David said in Psalms 3:11…
Junior Bishop II: That would be King Solomon.
JB I [stroking beard]: 27cm of beard says it was King David.
JB II [fingering 23cm of beard with defeated look]: I can't argue against such great reasoning.

And there would be peace in the church; thousands of believers would turn to us.

If we wanted to impress people with our powers, we wouldn't do that healing thing. We'd hire the wire technicians who worked on *The Matrix* trilogy. The marquee would be packed with 20,000 people singing songs about our general sacredness and we'd arrive through the sunroof, white robes flapping in the wind. They'd be so impressed they'd pay us another ten per cent without us asking. Our cup would truly runneth over. Those guys with tiny hats and flowing robes in the Vatican would have to come with some creative ideas to curb the flow of worshippers from their own church to ours. But the masses would still convert in droves and the Vatican guys would have to begrudgingly admit defeat.

At this point we'd start displaying the great competence and good business practice and stuff we have learnt in the corporate world. We'd

The Church Of Thirst And The Beard

start planning a hostile takeover of that entire Vatican place. We would point out the obvious flaws in their set up – like the fact that neither the previous Pope nor the current one kept a beard. As a result of our effective infomercials, the general public would be sold on the divinity of a full beard and they would be appalled. The Vatican would have to release an unplanned epistle defending themselves, quoting liberally from Scripture and medieval texts.

Of course, they would be playing right into our hands. We'd be expecting this move. We would then publicise the discovery of an ancient lost Gospel – the Gospel of the Beard. It would be a fake but by this time nobody would care enough to authenticate it. At this point the mass media would be in full feeding frenzy. The newspapers would be flooded with catchy sound bites such as "No beard, no heaven". People would be going berserk. Instead of a TV slot like Ray McCauley and those other unbearded guys, we'd go straight to the big screen. We'd do a full-length three-hour epic feature starring an assortment of great bearded actors – actors like Chuck Norris. The pay-off line for the movie trailer would be, "Chuck wears a full beard. Shouldn't you?"

Tell me you wouldn't join my church.

The Church Of Thirst And The Beard

Acknowledgments

It is impossible to stress the importance of recognising those individuals who play a critical role in my support structure. Without the following people, I'd be, as I like pointing out, like John the Baptist wandering the wilderness, munching on locusts and mumbling unintelligible gibberish. Well, more than I normally do, in any case.

The Men of Thirst (a.k.a. the MOT): you are the vicious, uncouth bastards who engage with me on a daily basis and serve only one purpose; viz, to deflate my runaway ego by consistently hurling insults at me. Shut up and let's drink diz here beers! The Sumo, Dark Lord, King Dogg the Anti-Christ, Battyboy, Bouga Two, Khaladi 0.5 and Ntshings. Ditto the MOT tea ladies: Zama and Stha. We few! We happy few! We band of savage brothers!

There are also "industry" people who, for reasons best known to them, have been more than generous with their time, energy and brains in nurturing whatever miniscule nuggets of talent I have inside of me. They are the people who have ensured that I keep plodding on in the general direction of whatever my full potential is:

Fred Khumalo (*Abafe abathakathi Mzilikazi!*); Sandile Ngidi (*Mfanakithi wathathwaphi?*); the TOM peeps, Rob, Akin and Kgomotso (Shine Shorty, shine!); Sarah Britten (We shall insult them on the beaches! We shall insult them on the blogs!); Zukiswa Wanner (Comrade Chic-lit, just one more and you're an author...); Jihan El-Tahri (My Egyptian charm, we'll always have Polokwane!); Masechaba Moshoeshoe (Fifteen years on, we're still engaged in conversation, albeit minus Mokoena).

My family-in-law who have adopted this stray mutt from the Valley as one of their own: Koko Ntsoeng, Rakgolo Malesela, Mam' Tshidi – *"Le gole gole, empa le se ke la lekana le ditlou"*. My other "siblings", Mpho, Thabang and *mpintshi ya ka* Aus' Sophie.

My sisters who know me more than most people ever will, Sinenhlanhla Ndimande and Khanyi Mjwara. *Nikhule kodwa ningakhokhobi bo weMwelase noS'shosho!*

And my (still) unflappable rock, my Northern Star and personal GPS, my soulmate and wife, Tebogo Ngcobo. Still getting down!

ALSO BY TWO DOGS...

Some Of My Best Friends Are White
By Ndumiso Ngcobo

Crossing various controversial, amusing and downright confusing racial divides, *Some Of My Best Friends Are White* delivers a healthy dose of black – and white – humour as it explores some of the Rainbow Nation's defining characteristics and many colourful characters, from minibus taxis to township life to AA choices to white people's team-building exercises… Ndumiso Ngcobo's debut book – a collection of satirical essays on contemporary South African issues from the point of view of a successful corporate professional who just happens to be Zulu – was released in 2007 and quickly became a widely acclaimed best-seller. It was shortlisted for the Neilsen Bookseller's Choice Award 2008.

"A hilarious collection of ballsy, in-your-face writing… Ndumiso Ngcobo is PJ O'Rourke with too much melanin and minus the jingoistic tendencies. His humour is effortless as he peppers you machine-gun style with the home truths of a township raconteur" – *Fred Khumalo*

ISBN 9781920137182

Is It Just Me Or Is Everything Still Kak? 2Kak 2Furious

By Tim Richman & Grant Schreiber

The best-selling sequel to *Is It Just Me Or Is Everything Kak?* continues where the first book left off, cataloguing the never-ending kakness of our times. Fresh topics include Afrikaans music, Julius Malema, Hermanus, Portaloos, Tom Cruise, Facebook, Robert Mugabe, gas braais, Kevin Pietersen, Valentine's Day and more…

"An absolute hoot… These guys are our version of the acerbic British columnists Jeremy Clarkson and AA Gill" – *Saturday Dispatch*

ISBN 9781920137267

Other books by Two Dogs:

293 Things Every SA Man Should Know
Modern Man Is A Wimp…
Why I'll Never Live In Oz Again
Some Of My Best Friends Are White
Defending The Caveman
Is It Just Me Or Is Everything Kak?
25 Cars To Drive Before You Die
Is It Just Me Or Is Everything Still Kak?
Is Dit Net Ek Of Is Als Tos?
Beat The Crunch!

FOR MORE INFORMATION ON TWO DOGS VISIT
www.twodogs.co.za